EASY BREASTFEEDING

All you need to know to give your baby the best possible start.

CAMILLA CONTI

HEALTH HARMONY

B. Jain Publishers (P) Ltd.
An ISO 9001:2000 Certified Company
USA - EUROPE - INDIA

EASY BREASTFEEDING

First Edition: 2010
Ist Impression: 2010

All rights reserved. No part of this book may be reproduced, stored in a retrieval system or transmitted, in any form or by any means, mechanical, photocopying, recording or otherwise, without any prior written permission of the publisher.

© with the author

Published by Kuldeep Jain for

An imprint of
B. JAIN PUBLISHERS (P) LTD.
An ISO 9001 : 2000 Certified Company
1921/10, Chuna Mandi, Paharganj, New Delhi 110 055 (INDIA)
Tel.: 91-11-4567 1000
Fax: 91-11-4567 1010 • *Email:* info@bjain.com
Website: **www.bjainbooks.com**

Cover design & layout: Vijesh Chahal

Printed in India by
J.J. OFFSET PRINTERS

ISBN: 978-81-319-0962-1

Dedicated to my children who taught me the real truth and essence of breastfeeding – love.

Acknowledgements

I sincerely thank Dr Arun Gupta for his support and patience when revising my work. I also thank the Breastfeeding Promotion Network of India for the images that they have allowed me to use in this book.

Many thanks to La Leche League Italia, to Elena, Manuela and Roberta for the beautiful pictures that they agreed to share.

A special 'thank you' to all my dear ones who gave company to my children while I was working and have always encouraged me and supported me, not only in writing this book but during my own breastfeeding experience.

Thanks to all the beautiful women who taught me something about breastfeeding, especially Karen, Tiziana and Paola.

Introduction

I was twenty five years old when my first child was born – a pretty young age by today's standards, at least in the so called western countries.

I had a degree in education and lots of work experience in the care of grown up children, but almost no clue about how to deal with a newborn.

In today's globalized, spread out societies, the disintegration of the extended family leaves us without that whole range of experiences which used to expose different generations to each other. So the young might learn from the elder and vice versa.

We hardly see a child being breastfed – and sometimes we hardly see a child in our immediate family setting at all.

Once upon a time children used to learn by taking care of siblings, cousins and nephews, by seeing their mothers and relatives taking care of them. Nowadays women often become mothers without ever having held a baby long enough to learn how to understand his clues.

Commercial interests, which rule our lives evermore, build up our imagery of care. We are much more familiar with the idea of a baby drinking from a bottle or sleeping with a pacifier in his mouth, than with the content, peaceful expression painted on one who's just fallen asleep suckling his mother's breast.

Some of us might even feel uncomfortable with the idea of babies nursing from breasts. We may be concerned about showing a part of our body or about our body changing shape.

We ignore the cost of not using an organ for the function it was meant for. Sometimes our own mothers have not breast fed us, convinced by the boom of industrialisation that somehow artificial must be better than natural.

Why? In an era when practical example is missing and women are – in spite of the emancipation that we claim - victims of commercial interests that subtly discourage breastfeeding, I had the luck of seeing my mom breastfeeding my twelve-years-younger-than-me sister. It looked so natural, so normal that frankly I have never contemplated any alternative.

This was not my only luck – because yes, what was once the norm has now become a rare privilege!

I somehow found the right people at the right moment. Starting with a superb midwife who once told me that "delivering is such a fun experience" and who said, in her self-presentation during the prenatal class she was holding, that she had breastfed her first child for three years and her second one for two and a half.

Woah! I loved her. She disclosed a world in front of my young inexperienced eyes. It seemed possible. I cheered up a bit from the discomfort of seeing around me so many women who could not succeed in breastfeedng.

How could it be that suddenly, after years of human evolution and perfecting of the mechanism, nature started failing so badly?

I got the clue that it could not be that way. My mother in law breastfed five children, the last of whom for five years! And most village women around the world breastfeed, too. Even malnourished Sub-saharan women seem to have enough milk supply for their babies. They often feed more than one baby at a time and those children thrive – and they actually often survive only because of that precious mother's milk.

So what is this myth of us – well fed and healthy city women not having milk – all about? Other constraints must be there.

These lay in the power of milk industries, which slowly made us forget our "womanly art", in the medicalisation of birth and in the disempowerment of women (yes, we are being expropriated of our birthing and mothering experience!). We have often no say in our babies' upbringing choices (there is always someone's voice who seems to count more, may it be that of doctors and experts or of parents and in-laws). Many women have no choice but to bottle-feed, because they need to work and they have no maternity leave, neither appropriate pauses for breastfeeding nor facilities to express their milk and send it to their babies.

I had the luck of being stubborn, of having a family who is tremendously respectful of my choices and of finding competent help to guide me during the first weeks of breastfeeding.

I had the luck of a natural delivery (so many caesarians and operative deliveries are nowadays being performed without any real need!), with no complications and I was never separated from my child.

Not every woman is as lucky as I. Unfortunately, very few are. That is why this book. After three years of nursing my daughter I had a second baby and now I am nursing them both. My milk is perfectly sufficient for two, like any woman's would be, with proper experience and maybe just a bit of help.

This is not to say that everyone should do the same, neither to engage in a race on who can breastfeed more children at once. What I want to tell you is: you can! Actually almost every mother can. Cases of women not having enough milk are really rare and even in those cases some milk is there: better giving little than nothing!

After getting interested in breastfeeding issues, I started studying to help others to succeed too and researching more and more on the topic. When Jain House asked me to write this book I was very excited to use the knowledge that I was gaining to other women's benefit.

Every information here presented is the fruit of a careful and passionate research from the teachings of breastfeeding experts, people who deal every day with breastfeeding mothers and babies and help them to find solutions to their problems.

I do not mean to indoctrinate or force my point of view on anyone. But yes, I take a stand: I do consider breast milk superior to any other kind of infant food.

And I simply wish you to enjoy the breastfeeding relationship with your babies the way I do.

Just a note: having to take a decision on a formal matter, I have resolved to refer to the baby as a 'he'. This is not because of any masculine preference, but just for simplicity and clarity. Since the book mainly talks about babies and mothers and the mother definitely has to be a 'she'.

With best wishes to all of you,

Camilla Conti

Publisher's Note

The relation of a mother and child is a unique, incomparable relation. From the moment of conception, a mother and her child gets bonded in a strange bond of love and faith.

This book 'Easy Breastfeeding' comes at a crucial time when there is no guidance from elders as it used to be in the joint families and when mothers are shying away from feeding their children; when feeding bottles are sadly taking the place of breastfeeding. Written with a lot of emotion, this book will serve as a guide to new mothers and enlighten and empower them on this very serious and necessary subject. It also helps them to understand how their body works and also dispels myths about many old beliefs providing a clear understanding of this beautiful process of breastfeeding, its utility and its amazing consequences on a newborn.

The author has passionately written on this issue with a purpose. She wishes to awaken all new mothers and would-be-mothers to this great responsibility that they hold towards their infants who have just come into this world!

- Kuldeep Jain
CEO, B. Jain Publishers (P) Ltd.

Foreword

This is one of the books with a very clear understanding of the subject of breastfeeding and complementary feeding. While it provides sufficient guidance on why breastfeeding, more importantly it helps to empower women with the art of breastfeeding and making them successful in achieving the optimal feeding practices of their infants. Exclusive breastfeeding for the first six months is a health recommendation of the World Health Organization and other technical bodies. It requires a good degree of support to women to be able to provide this to their babies. This could be maternity leave of structural support for mothers and babies to stay together, especially during the first six months of life. Thereafter, babies need solid family foods along with continued breastfeeding till two years or beyond. Information that breastfeeding is controlled by a hormonal cycle is very relevant. This is critical to the success of breastfeeding. If all women could learn that 'not enough milk' for the baby is more of a perception and feeling but it leads to depressed flow of their own milk, it could make the desired difference. Apart from the health system support that a mother needs, the book provides interesting information about how to spot a breastfeeding friendly doctor or a hospital. The first weeks are of particular importance. It is a time to learn and to know each other, and 'every baby is unique'. Introduction of complementary feeding, when and what food to be given, is very nicely dealt with. Touching upon few problems faced by mothers and children is a helpful guide though some of them require good medical attention. Readers of this book, I am sure would find it very interesting and feel empowered to demand good services from their health systems and governments to support breastfeeding. Reading will surely contribute to better health and development of your children !

- Dr Arun Gupta, MD, FIAP,
Regional Coordinator,
International Baby Food Action Network (IBFAN) Asia.
Member, Prime Minister's Council on India's Nutrition Challenges.
Member, Steering Committee, World Alliance for Breastfeeding Action (WABA)

Contents

Dedication	iii
Acknowledgements	v
Introduction	vii
Publisher's note	xi
Foreword	xiii

1. WHY BREASTFEEDING? — 01-04
- What makes the difference? — 01
- Advantages for the baby — 02
- Advantages for the mother — 02
- Practical difficulties, false myths and bad advices about breast feeding — 03
- Formula milk in comparison to breast milk — 03

2. BREAST ANATOMY AND MILK PRODUCTION — 05-07
- Regulation and release of milk production by specific hormones — 06

3. PREGNANCY – A TIME TO GET READY — 08-15
- Use this time to acquire information — 08
- Build your support network — 08
- Plan your delivery — 09
- Distinguishing valid counselors from bad advisors — 10

4. DELIVERY AND THERE ABOUT — 16-23
- A natural delivery is always desirable — 16
- Breastfeeding within an hour of delivery proves beneficial — 16
- Learning proper latching and positioning — 17
- Loss of the baby's weight during the first three-four days — 17
- A caesarian section or an operative delivery — 18
- A delayed beginning — 18
- Abstain from giving water and glucose to a newborn — 18
- Unrestricted feedings — 19
- Free formula samples and advertisements — 19

5. THE VERY FIRST DROPS... — 24-25
- Importance of colostrum — 24

6.	**BIRTH OF LOVE**	**26-28**
	• Developing a bond with the baby	26
7.	**AND HERE WE START**	**29-33**
	• Importance of a good latching	29
	• Shape and size do not matter	33
8.	**BREASTFEEDING MANAGEMENT**	**34-38**
	• Positions	34
	• Forget the clock	34
	• Growth sprints	36
	• Taking out the nipple from the baby's mouth	36
	• Recognizing your baby's hunger signals	37
	• The first weeks	37
	• Optimal duration of breastfeeding	38
9.	**EVERY BABY IS UNIQUE**	**39-40**
	• How well do you know your baby?	39
10.	**BABIES' GROWTH**	**41-43**
	• Method to know if your child is getting enough milk	41
	• Normal growth parameters	42
	• Percentiles, percentiles…	43
11.	**WHEN THE BABY IS NOT GETTING ENOUGH MILK…**	**44-48**
	• Improving your breastfeeding technique	44
	• Breast compression	45
	• Herbal remedies	45
	• Domperidone	46
	• Alternative supplementation techniques	46
	• Alternative methods to give supplements	46
12.	**COMMON PROBLEMS AND THEIR TREATMENTS**	**49-56**
	• Baby's problems	49
	• Babies on a strike	51
	• The biter	52
	• Mother's problems	52
13.	**MOTHER'S NUTRITION**	**57-58**
14.	**GETTING REST**	**59-60**
15.	**BREASTFEEDING AND CONTRACEPTION**	**61-61**
	• Lactation Amenorrhea Method (LAM)	61

- Other contraceptive methods — 61

16. BREASTFEEDING AND PHYSICAL ACIVITY — 62-62

17. MILK EXPRESSION — 63-65
- When it is needed — 63
- When it is not needed — 63
- Manual expression — 64
- Pumps — 64
- Tips to facilitate milk expression — 65
- How to preserve and use expressed milk — 65

18. SPECIAL CIRCUMSTANCES — 66-72
- Twins — 66
- Pregnancy and tandem nursing — 67
- Caesarian and operative deliveries — 68
- Premature babies — 69
- Kangaroo care — 69
- Newborn jaundice — 70
- Newborn hypoglycemia — 71
- Genetic and metabolic problems — 71

19. WHEN THE MOTHER HAS MEDICAL PROBLEMS — 73-73

20. READY FOR THE FIRST COMPLEMENTARY FOODS — 74-76
- When is the right time? — 74
- Signs to watch out for — 74
- Complementing, not substituting! — 75
- What are the right foods? — 75
- A note about allergies and intolerances — 76

21. BREASTFEEDING OLDER CHILDREN — 77-77

22. WEANING — 78

23. BIBLIOGRAPHY — 80

Why Breastfeeding?

What makes the difference?

Breastfeeding is the normal way of feeding babies and it makes a difference for your baby and for yourself in terms of physical and psychological well-being. Breast-milk is specific for human babies, the product of millennia of evolution, perfectly designed to meet the demands of their rapidly growing brain. It contains all the nutrients for the optimal brain development and other physical growth needs mixed just in the right proportion according to each stage of babies' growth. Cow's milk and formulas remain identical to each other. Mother's milk is an ever changing food, always altering to meet the child's needs—week by week, month by month, year by year and even in the course of the same nursing session!

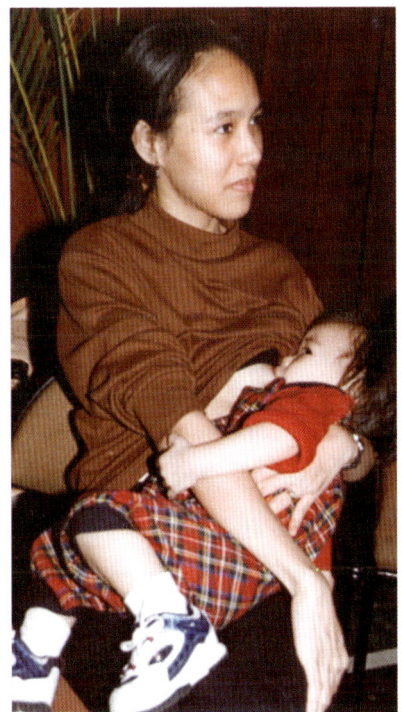

The ever changing quality of mother's milk exposes the baby to different tastes. When solids are introduced, the child is generally eager to explore to try new foods (especially those that are present in his mother's diet). And this is just one of the advantages of breastfeeding.

Source: BPNI's Training Material "Infant and Young Child Feeding Counseling: A Training Course - The 3 in 1 course"

Advantages for the baby

Mother's milk contains nutrients that enhance the immunity of the baby thus saving the baby from infections. These are even more effective when the baby exclusively receives breast-milk and their protection becomes stronger when breastfeeding is prolonged.

There seems to be a positive correlation between breastfeeding and higher IQ in children, especially if breastfeeding is prolonged. This can be due to two reasons—the special composition of mother's milk (it contains everything your baby needs in the right proportion: carbohydrates, lipids, proteins, minerals, vitamins, hormones, growth factors, white globules and anti-inflammatory factors, water) and to the higher degree of physical touch received by the breastfed children.

Breastfeeding promotes optimal development of jaws and facial muscles, because of the peculiar suction motion required to nurse from the breast, which is different than drinking from a bottle.

Advantages for the mother

Tuning yourself with your baby

The peculiar hormonal condition of the breastfeeding mother (high levels of prolactin and oxytocin) makes her very responsive to her child's clues and somehow more capable to satisfy his needs. There is a positive cycle of satisfaction, in a mutual reinforcement which helps the mother feel suitable to her new role and at the height of ability needed for the task. This can significantly prevent syndromes like postpartum depression or baby blues. The same hormones have a tranquilizing effect and help the mother relax and recover from delivery.

Breastfeeding a baby often works better than a sleeping pill especially when you feed your baby and lie next to him or her. Some women feel that one hour of sleep while breastfeeding is just as refreshing as five without breastfeeding. This is very important during the first weeks after the delivery as breastfeeding gives you special moments for yourself, to touch your baby, to rest or listen to music, to read a book… Breastfeeding does require a lot of time and commitment by the mother, but ultimately much time is saved from sterilizing bottles, nipples and other accessories. Breast-milk is always ready, always at the right temperature and it does not require any more cleaning than the normal daily mother hygiene. This makes it also very practical in case of traveling. You do not have to worry about carrying anything, neither about finding a proper place to clean and sterilize bottles or to warm the milk.

Working mothers and breastfeeding
If the mother is a working woman but breastfeeds her child, her child will fall sick less times and the mother will miss less number of working days. Moreover, nursing is helpful to reconnect after being separated from the baby. It is something special that no baby-sitter or other caregiver can do. Breastfeeding also helps in recovering optimal shape after birth by loosing the extra weight accumulated with pregnancy (fat stored by the body during pregnancy is in fact meant to be a provision for breastfeeding). It prevents breast cancer (the protective effect of breastfeeding grows along with its duration) and future osteoporosis *too*. It has been seen that women who have breastfed recover more quickly of the bone density lost during pregnancy.

Practical difficulties, false myths and bad advices about breast feeding

Breastfeeding is the most normal way to feed a child and the natural consequence of pregnancy and delivery. Your body has been taking care of your child's nutrition while he was in uterus. In the same way nature provided you all that you need to breastfeed your baby. Cases in which a woman is really incapable to breastfeed are extremely rare. Most breastfeeding problems can be prevented or solved with a bit of practical help and patience. And even in those very few circumstances in which a woman cannot produce enough milk to satisfy her baby's needs totally, expressed or donated human milk is better to use other than any tinned baby food.

Formula milk in comparison to breast milk

It is in fact inferior, but it is always identical, in its chemical composition and taste. During the manufacturing of it serious mistakes may occur which can be dangerous! There is a high risk of contamination too.

There have been countless scandals on this issue which have caught the media's attention when contaminated formula powders killed or impaired thousands of infants. In poorer countries, thousands of children have been falling sick because of formula milk prepared with contaminated water or due to the lack of sterile conditions.

Besides the risk of contamination, formula milk does not provide immunity from infections, which on the contrary comes with mother milk. Risks of artificial feeding, which are so evident in poorer environmental backgrounds, are nevertheless not absent for children belonging to richer social strata or areas of the world. Contamination and mistakes in the preparation are always a possibility. Furthermore artificially fed infants are exposed to higher risks of respiratory infections, neonatal meningitis, septicemia, ear infection, diarrhea and gastrointestinal infections, necrotizing enterocolitis (especially the premature baby), urinary infections, diabetes, obesity, cardiovascular diseases, asthma and allergies, orthodontic problems and even certain types of childhood cancer may also occur. Some studies show a positive *correlation between artificial feeding and crib deaths* (SIDS, Sudden Infant Death Syndrome). This could be due to the fact that breastfed babies often sleep closer to their mother, but also to the protection that breastfeeding offers from infections.

Many women choose not to breastfeed because they worry about the loss of toning of their breasts. But breasts are in any case going to change their shape as an effect of aging and pregnancy and not only breastfeeding. If such changes are natural in women, then what is the use of not using an organ for a purpose for which it has been designed! And especially if it is something so special and so important for our children's health – isn't it worth enough? There is a higher risk of anemia in women who do not breastfeed, because breastfeeding helps the uterus to contract and recover its normal shape and dimension quickly. This reduces bleeding after delivery.

There is a higher risk of early pregnancies for non breastfeeding women, since breastfeeding, when specific conditions are met (see: *Breastfeeding and contraception*), postpones ovulation and helps spacing out children. Last but not least, artificial feeding costs, breast milk is free!

Breast Anatomy and Milk Production

Breasts are secretory glands formed of different tissues.

The **glandular tissue** starts with the *alveoli*, where milk is synthesized from blood. These are grouped in clusters called *lobes* and *lobules* and connected to a series of *ducts* and *ductules*, which are ramified like the branches of a tree. They are the channels through which milk flows towards the nipple. The alveoli are surrounded by myoepithelial cells, which contract and push the milk in the ducts when stimulated by oxytocin hormone (*let-down or ejection reflex*). The **connective tissue** is formed of linkages which support the breast. The **adipose tissue** gives shape and dimension to the breast and protects it from injury.

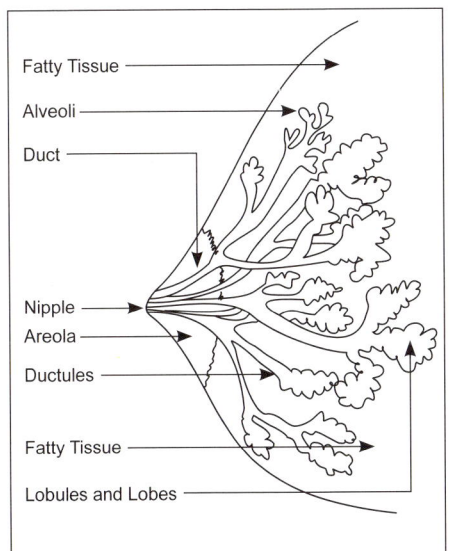

As you can see, dimension and shape have nothing to do with the capacity to produce milk.

Blood vessels provide the necessary substances to synthesize milk. **Nerves** make breasts sensitive to the baby's suction. They pass information to the brain which will give the command to release hormones responsible for the let down or ejection reflex. The **lymphatic system** eliminates waste substances.

The **nipple**, which protrudes from a round, dark portion of pigmented skin called **areola**, has five to ten openings through which milk flows to the baby's mouth. It is made of muscular tissue which contracts when stimulated and it is flexible and adjustable to the baby's mouth.

Small pimply-like glands, the **Montgomery glands**, are located on the areola. These become bigger during pregnancy and their function is to lubrify and disinfect the area to prevent bacteria from multiplying (that is why disinfecting breast is not necessary; washing them once a day with neutral soap is more than enough).

Regulation and release of milk production by specific hormones

During pregnancy some hormonal changes prepare the breasts for breastfeeding. After the baby is born, *prolactin hormone* will be responsible for milk production. Prolactin levels in the blood are very high immediately after delivering. Later they slowly decrease, although they remain higher in lactating women. When the baby's suction stimulates the breast, the network of nerves from the nipple area passes the information to the brain and prolactin is released. The release of this hormone stimulates the *alveoli* to produce milk. *Prolactin levels in the blood rise every time the baby nurses or the mother expresses milk.* They reach their peak approximately forty-five minutes after nursing and especially between 2 and 6 am. This is a response to the intense and frequent nursing during the night but it could also be due to the fact that prolactin works better in the absence of light and that the mother is more relaxed during night time. This is the reason why it is very important to nurse the baby frequently and especially during the night in order to maintain a good milk supply or in case there is a need to increase it. Since prolactin is so deeply connected with motherhood, it is also referred to as 'the hormone of maternity'. Prolactin release is inhibited by smoke and by the *Prolactin Inhibiting Factor* (PIF). The PIF acts when breasts are not emptied, passing the message to the brain that new milk should not be produced. Again we see how a high frequency of nursing prevents milk supply from dropping down.

The let-down or ejection reflex is activated by *oxytocin hormone*. This stimulates the contraction of the alveoli, which expel milk towards

Breast Anatomy and Milk Production

the nipple, through ductules and ducts. Since oxytocin also stimulates uterine contractions (it is responsible for the proceeding of labor and delivery), it has a very important role in bringing the uterus back to its normal dimension after birth. When the baby sucks, the release of oxytocin causes the uterus to contract. This is why immediately after delivery the woman may feel some kind of contraction-like belly pain while nursing. It is a normal phenomenon which disappears after few days and it is very important for the mother's recovery after birth.

Oxytocin release and the let-down reflex can happen even without physical stimulation. It may happen by being in direct physical contact with the baby, touching him, hearing his cry, smelling him and even just looking at his photograph or thinking of him. It is not rare for a mother to see milk leaking from her breasts as she thinks that it is almost time to nurse her baby.

Oxytocin release can be inhibited by stress, tiredness, doubts, lack of confidence, pain (ex. sore breasts or episiotomy pain), and separation from the child, scarce or absent skin to skin touch.

The Italian prenatal educator Piera Maghella calls it the 'shy hormone': if the woman feels judged or invaded in her privacy it will not be released. Oxytocin release can be facilitated by privacy, relaxation, deep breathing, rest and self pampering, breast or back massage, a hot bath or a shower, warm applications on the breasts etc. This is why you should remain confident about yourself and breastfeeding that will help stimulate oxytocin and enhance your own milk supply.

CHART 1
A USEFUL MASSAGE TO STIMULATE OXYTOCIN RELEASE

While the mother sits comfortably, her back bent forward, gently massage her with circular movements, all along her spine on both sides.

Pregnancy – A Time to Get Ready

Use this time to acquire information
Read all that you can about breastfeeding. Search on books and websites. Attend specific seminars or support groups, like those organized by La Leche League International or other health groups or institutions present in your area (see chart 2). Meeting women who are already breastfeeding, seeing breastfed children of different ages can be really useful.

Build your support network
Find people who can help you in case of breastfeeding problems (see breastfeeding resources listed in chart 2 and find out what is available in your area). Search out for mothers with positive breastfeeding experiences or who could successfully overcome breastfeeding difficulties. Mind that not all health care personnel (gynecologists, pediatricians, nurses, midwives…) are really prepared on breastfeeding issues. Bad advices risk the success of breastfeeding. It is important to build up your own knowledge on the subject, to be prepared and secure enough to make your point of view stand in case any problem arises.

Organize a network of practical help around you for the first period after delivery. This does not mean, like most well meaning grandmothers and aunties intend it, having other people become substitute mothers for your baby, "so that you can rest". It is much more helpful for you and your newborn to have time to know each other and learn breastfeeding. Others can help you by preparing your food, taking care of household chores, going for grocery, looking after older children.

Plan your delivery

After acquiring adequate knowledge on breastfeeding, we suggest to make an informed choice about the place where you will deliver your baby.

Look out for the place that will allow you to establish a good breastfeeding relationship with your baby and get a good start.

Look for a birth team who is supportive to breastfeeding, who will not separate you from your baby after delivery and during the days that you will spend in the hospital. 'Rooming in' should be allowed. For example, the baby should be all day and night near his mother, so that he will be able to nurse whenever he needs.

You may be interested to know that, in case of good health condition of the baby and the mother (after a proper medical checkup), the mother can normally sign an informed consent form where she takes charge of the responsibility and she is allowed to leave the hospital before the standard three days or whatever is the routine of that hospital. No milk supplement or glucose water should be given unless real emergency arises.

You can discuss all these and other issues of your concern during visits in the hospital before delivering and you can eventually write them down in a birth plan. This is a letter to be signed in two or more copies, one to be carried with you when you reach the hospital for the delivery and the others to be given to the person who will assist you.

Since you might be in a particular emotional and psychological condition at the moment of delivering, it is useful to have your needs known and supported by the person who will assist you during the delivery, may that be your partner or another person of your choice.

It could be a *doula* or childbirth assistance, if this service is available. Whosoever you chose, he or she should be your advocate.

Discuss your needs with this person in advance; make sure he or she knows how important breastfeeding is for you and for your child and how you want to go about it. Discuss and plan strategies for special circumstances. For example, if an emergency or a caesarian section occurs or the baby is born premature.

If you are expecting twins or more, your support network and delivery should be planned even more carefully, so that you will be able to get the most relaxed environment and the best breastfeeding support that you can.

You do not need to prepare your nipples for breastfeeding by rubbing them or by any other strange torture. It can hurt you and it does not help preventing pain or cracks while nursing. Pain can only be prevented or eliminated by correct latching.

Distinguishing valid counselors from bad advisors

The pediatrician Jack Newman, one of the most expert lactation consultants and breastfeeding researchers in North America, gives us some directions on how to recognize health professionals who do not support breastfeeding (in spite of perhaps openly saying that they do not). Such bad advisors might recommend specific formula brands or distribute infant feeding literature made by formula companies; they might give the same value to breast milk and formula. They might tell you that it is not necessary to breastfeed the baby immediately after birth, since you will be too tired and the baby is often not interested anyway. They might tell you that there is no such thing as nipple confusion and that you should start giving bottles early to make sure the baby will accept the bottle nipple; they might discourage breastfeeding in case of maternal or baby's illness or be surprised to learn that your 6 months old baby is still breastfeeding. They might tell you that there is no value in breast milk after the baby reaches a certain age; they might also tell you that you must never allow your baby to fall asleep at the breast, not to stay in the hospital to breastfeed your sick child because it is important for you to rest at home.

False myths regarding breastfeeding can come from anyone—friends, relatives who may have unsuccessful breastfeeding stories behind them or carry out dated prejudices. Some people just cannot resist distributing advices to new mothers. We will only give one suggestion. Learn from your own notions and experiences.

CHART 2
SOME USEFUL RESOURCES ON BREASTFEEDING

Here are some resources to build up your knowledge on breastfeeding and related issues.

Books:

LLLI, THE WOMANLY ART OF BREASTFEEDING

Bumgarner, Norma Jane, MOTHERING YOUR NURSING TODDLER

Gonzales, Carlos, MY CHILD WON'T EAT!

Newman, Jack & Teresa Pitman, THE ULTIMATE BREASTFEEDING BOOK OF ANSWERS

Sears, William, NIGHTTIME PARENTING

Sears, William & Martha Sears, THE BABY BOOK

Organizations and websites where you can find breastfeeding support and be addressed to prepared lactation consultants:

La Leche League international (www.llli.org) is a volunteer, no profit organization offering mother to mother support for breastfeeding through support groups and very prepared breastfeeding consultants. It produces several publications on breastfeeding and it gives online or telephonic help. It organizes seminars on breastfeeding issues. It is present in several areas of the world and it is an extremely useful resource for breastfeeding mothers.

The International baby Food Action Network (www.ibfan.org) is a worldwide network of public interest groups with the aim of reducing infant and young children morbidity and mortality, promoting breastfeeding and optimal nutrition practices. It has different branches in several areas of the world.

The same aim is pursued by the Breastfeeding Promotion Network of India (www.bpni.org).

The International lactation consultant association (www.ilca.org) is a worldwide network of International Board Certified Lactation Consultants (IBCLCs) and other health care professionals working with breastfeeding families. It offers several resources and publications on breastfeeding.

The World Alliance for Breastfeeding Action (www.waba.org.my) is again an international organization that offers support to protect and promote breastfeeding.

Other websites:

www.breastfeeding.com (general information on breastfeeding)

www.breastfeedingonline.com (information and resources on breastfeeding)

www.thebirthden.com/Newman.html (Doctor Jack Newman's website: videos and a lot of useful material)

www.kellymom.com/nursingtwo/faq/index.html (about tandem nursing)

www.breastfed.com (information and researches on breastfeeding related issues)

www.promom.org (it promotes awareness and acceptance of breastfeeding)

CHART 3
THE 'MOTHER ASSISTANT'

Doula (also known as 'mother assistant' or 'childbirth assistant') is a Greek word, which means "the one who serves the woman". She is a childbirth education professional who assists and accompanies the woman through pregnancy, delivery and the first period of life with the newborn.

Traditionally in every culture women have been assisted by other women during pregnancy, delivery and postpartum.

This important source of support is being lost in modern societies, where nuclear family is becoming the norm. Health care structures rarely follow up women after delivery and rarely do they offer the kind of emotional and personalized support that is needed during pregnancy and delivery itself. Women miss the experienced help and reassurance of being near someone who has already gone through birth experience and now is there for them (for their physical and emotional needs, to encourage and reassure them, to help them become mothers).

Here comes the *doula*, who is not meant to be a nurse for the baby or a substitute mother, but a support to the mother. Her role is to empower women in their motherhood experience. The mother needs to be protagonist of her own delivery experience and baby's care, in order to be happy. She needs to be helped to feel capable and at the height of the task. This is a powerful prevention for post partum depression syndromes and *baby blues*.

The *doula* generally meets the mother few times during pregnancy, she may teach her relaxation techniques or exercises, positions for delivery, etc. She may give her advices regarding small problems related to her pregnancy. She may help the mother or the couple to write down their needs in a delivery plan. She accompanies parents during all phases of labor and delivery, assisting with encouragement, massage and other non pharmacological forms of pain relief (note that she is not entitled to perform a medical role!). She is the advocate of parents' needs and she can mediate, if need be, with health care personnel and bureaucracy. She supports the partner so that he can better support the woman.

She facilitates initiation of breastfeeding immediately after delivery and she helps latching the baby correctly and establishing a successful breastfeeding relationship during the first weeks after birth.

She supports the mother and the couple during the first weeks at home with the new baby. In a period of such intense physical and emotional changes, she can be a reassuring presence, someone to share doubts, fears, and worries with. She may even simply be a practical help in small daily activities like grocery or care of older children.

Lower incidence of postpartum depression and higher rate of successful breastfeeding experiences have been registered among women who availed the support of a *doula*.

You can find out if there is a *doula* service available in your area by browsing on internet, asking your hospital or a private or public center offering prenatal classes and childbirth education. You may enquire from breastfeeding resources like La Leche League International or others in your area.

CHART 4
BABY FRIENDLY HOSPITALS

The Baby Friendly Hospital Initiative (BFHI) was launched in 1991 by UNICEF and WHO to ensure adequate breastfeeding support in hospitals and maternity services.

In order to be awarded as 'Baby Friendly', maternity services need to follow ten specific steps:

- Have a written breastfeeding policy that is routinely communicated to all health care staff

- Train all health care staff in skills necessary to implement this policy
- Inform all pregnant women about the benefits and management of breastfeeding
- Help mothers initiate breastfeeding within one half-hour from birth
- Show mothers how to breastfeed and maintain lactation, even if they have to be separated from their infants
- Give newborn infants no food or drink other than breast milk unless medically indicated

Practice rooming in; that is, allow mothers and infants to remain together for a day

- Encourage breastfeeding on demand
- Give no artificial teats or pacifiers (also called dummies or soothers) to breastfeeding infants
- Foster the establishment of breastfeeding support groups and refer mothers to them on discharge from the hospital or clinic

(Source: http://www.unicef.org/programme/breastfeeding/baby.htm#10)

Following these indications can really make a difference to establish an environment which is conducive to successful breastfeeding. Several hospitals in different areas of the world have been awarded as Baby Friendly, although barriers remain to the full implementation of those ten steps. Choosing to deliver in a Child Friendly structure can help you to get a good start.

Delivery and there about

A natural delivery is always desirable

Natural deliveries (For example, vaginal deliveries, with no use of pharmacologic drugs like pain killers, epidural anesthesia or artificial oxytocin, and no maneuvers like forceps, episiotomy, etc.) make breastfeeding initiation easier. Babies who are not under the effect of medications given to the mother are more alert and willing to nurse and explore the breast. Drugs can make them sleepy and weak and they might not be in the mood of trying to nurse.

Painful procedures like episiotomies might leave the mother with extra pain and no immediate energy to be with her baby and nurse. The discomfort from episiotomies or other invasive maneuvers could also inhibit the oxytocin release that is so important to activate the let-down reflex and to bring the uterus back to its original dimension.

Breastfeeding within an hour of delivery proves beneficial

It has been seen that breastfeeding is more successful when started immediately after birth. After a natural delivery the baby is naturally willing to explore his mother's body and breast. This natural curiosity might be lost if the encounter is delayed. Babies who are separated from their mother after birth often become sleepy and uninterested in the breast.

Even in case they do not nurse properly at this time, they should be allowed to have a skin to skin nearness with their mother, lick and touch her nipples. It is noteworthy that they do not need to be taught or forced to latch on properly at that time.

If the mother is tired she can be helped to lie comfortably with her baby in her arms, resting on her chest. This is usually perceived as a fair reward after the tiring experience of delivering even in the cases where the delivery lasts for particularly a long time or was particularly painful. If the mother and baby need to be shifted into another room (because the delivery room is needed for someone else or because they need a warmer environment), it can be done without separating them. They can be wrapped together in a blanket and then moved, if heat is a concern.

Routine procedures like bathing, weight and height checking and other tests of the baby (like APGAR, etc.) can wait for a couple of hours without causing any risk to the newborn.

It has been seen that certain painful procedures on the baby (like suctioning) can make him loose interest in breastfeeding for some time. And in most cases they are not necessary! You can discuss these issues with a health care personnel before choosing the structure where you will deliver your baby.

Keep your baby close to you. Ask for 24 hours rooming in with your baby, which means having the baby with you day and night, so that you can develop a bond and give him your breast on demand, whenever he shows signs of hunger (see the specific paragraph on babies' signals of hunger).

Learning proper latching and positioning

It is the key to pain free nursing and it ensures that the baby will be able to empty the breasts. If you do not find competent personnel in the delivery place and you feel that you need help to learn latching or for any other problem do not hesitate to call a lactation expert.

Loss of the baby's weight during the first three-four days

A weight loss up to 5 to 7% of birth weight is normal. It is a consequence of the elimination of excess liquids after birth and the passage of first stools (meconium). The baby should regain his birth weight within ten to fifteen days from birth.

A caesarian section or an operative delivery

Breastfeeding is still possible, it may just require little more patience and competent help. After a caesarian delivery (especially if it was not planned), the mother might be left with the feeling of being inadequate, she might feel cheated by the structure or be angry with her baby, with her partner or with herself. She might be upset for the scar on her body or be in physical pain. In such special circumstances successful breastfeeding can be a compensation for the feeling of loss that delivery experience might have given her. It can ease the bonding with her baby and it will help her uterus to get back to its original size.

A delayed beginning

Do not get discouraged even in case if your baby is separated from you and the start is delayed. You can express your colostrum and milk and ask nurses or doctors to feed him with it. In this way, you will have a good supply when your baby will be ready to nurse and meanwhile he will also get the benefits of his mother's milk.

Abstain from giving water and glucose to a newborn

Do not give any formula, water or glucose water unless there is a real medical emergency. Even in case the baby is sleepy or not interested in nursing, dehydration is better prevented by encouraging him to nurse. Hypoglycemia is usually due to delayed or not frequent nursing.

Abstain form giving bottles and plastic nipples (pacifiers or dummies) Sucking from a bottle or pacifier is different than sucking from the breast. The baby might get confused, with the result that he will not be able to latch properly. Mothers' nipples will probably become sore or cracked and the baby might not get enough breast milk. Breasts could get engorged as a result of not being properly emptied and this can reduce milk supply.

Giving supplemental feedings can itself not allow breasts to be properly emptied and again engorgements will probably happen. Supplementing water or formula gives the baby a sense of satiety and it makes him less interested in nursing.

Water supplements expose the baby to a higher risk of jaundice, since he will get less of the laxative effect of colostrums and breast milk.

Formula supplements, being synthesized from cow milk, also expose babies to a higher risk of milk allergy or intolerance (because of the precocious exposure to cow milk proteins, which are made of longer chains of amino acids and are more difficult to digest compared to human milk proteins).

The use of pacifiers in order to delay feedings and keep the baby to a clock determined nursing schedule can also reduce milk supply. If breasts are not emptied according to babies' hunger, they will not produce the necessary amount of milk.

Furthermore an excessively hungry baby is likely to attack the breast with desperation and he will have no patience to wait for the mother to latch him correctly. This might create nipple pain.

Unrestricted feedings

No restriction on the frequency and duration of feedings should be imposed. This will help you build a good milk supply; new milk is produced when breasts are emptied. The laxative effect of colostrums and milk will also prevent or help to get rid of newborn jaundice.

Free formula samples and advertisements

Do not accept any free formula samples or advertisement by formula companies. You might be tempted to use them, if a problem arises. You should know that the use of formula even once can dislodge the practice of breastfeeding, which can be harmful. Distributing formula samples or advertising formulas violates the International Code on the Marketing of Breast milk Substitutes.

CHART 5
THE INTERNATIONAL CODE ON THE MARKETING OF BREAST MILK SUBSTITUTES.

The WHO and UNICEF International Code on the Marketing of Breast milk Substitutes was approved in 1981 by the **World Health Assembly** and the major companies producing baby food.

The Code was a response to the shocking infant deaths happening in the world as a consequence of substituting breast milk with infant formulas. Its aim is to protect breastfeeding by diffusing correct information on breastfeeding itself and preventing the advertisement of alternative infant foods.

The Code forbids the advertisement and promotion of bottles and plastic nipples, artificial formulas and any kind of baby food for children of age less than six months (biscuits, dry frozen or homogenized foods, herbal teas, or anything).

Advertisement and promotion of such products also refers to the distribution of free samples to new mothers and expectant mothers (they can only be distributed to doctors for scientific research) and distribution of gadgets, pamphlets with the logo or name of the company in the health care services.

Donations of equipment to health care services must be approved by government. They can have the logo or the name of the company but no mention of specific products must be there.

No donations or low cost sales can be done of the products included in the Code.

There should not be any kind of contact between mothers or expectant mothers and the representatives or employees of the baby food companies.

Any informational material distributed to families must clearly indicate the superiority of breast milk and the difficulty to step back after deciding to not breastfeed. Social and economic implication of not breastfeeding must be explained, along with the health risks of not breastfeeding.

Labels, brochures and pamphlets should not discourage breastfeeding in any open or subtle way. They must specify that the product should be used only under medical prescription and supervision.

Labels and brochures should avoid statements regarding health benefits of the products.

Governments and authorities should inform parents, childcare specialists and health care personnel that formulas are not sterile and there is a risk of contamination.

Every information should be written in the language spoken in the area where the product is being sold.

The Code has now value of law in several countries of the world. Nevertheless violations keep happening. The General Director of WHO produces periodical reports on the implementation of the Code, from which new resolutions are made to clarify and amplify the Code. These have the same value of the Code itself.

For further information you can visit the website of IBFAN (International Baby Food Action Network): www.ibfan.org

CHART 6
THE 'BREAST CRAWL'

Early initiation of breastfeeding offers many advantages for newborns and mothers. Immediately after birth babies are in a state of quite alertness which is very crucial for the establishment and duration of breastfeeding and to develop a bonding with their mother. Early initiation and skin to skin touch with their mother keep babies warm and expose them to the colonization of safe bacterial flora from mother's skin. This, together with colostrum (which has a high concentration of antibodies) protects them from infections.

Early initiation leads to better biochemical parameters (for example sugar levels) after birth and fastens the passage of meconium (first stool), reducing the intensity of physiological newborn jaundice.

There is evidence that the best way to initiate breastfeeding immediately after birth is what is known as the 'Breast Crawl'.

Like other mammals, even human babies have the capacity to reach their mother's breast and initiate breastfeeding without help, if they are not separated from their mother and they are allowed to experience skin to skin touch with her immediately after birth. This is at least valid for babies who are not under the effect of medications given to mothers during delivery. If care is taken while gently drying up the baby after birth, to leave the amniotic fluid on his hands, this familiar odour will drive him to his mother's breast.

Once the baby is put prone and skin to skin on his mother's stomach (from this position he can see her breasts and face), he will first start licking and sucking his own hands and then he will be attracted up towards his mother's nipples (as the smell of the substance secreted by nipples is similar to that of amniotic fluid).

The baby will start moving towards the nipples and then he will start touching, pinching them and liking them until he will finally hold the nipple in his mouth and start breastfeeding. The baby is also attracted by the darkness of the areola. His massage on the mother's nipples makes them protrude so that latching becomes easier. The same massage causes oxytocin release as well, which stimulates uterine contractions. Contractions (which are also stimulated by the baby's gentle kicks on mother's stomach) ease the expulsion of the placenta, diminishing bleeding and helping the uterus to get back to its original size.

The whole Breast Crawl process normally lasts thirty to sixty minutes, but it may take less time or longer may be longer time. It is important to leave mother and baby together skin to skin during these precious moments: they should not be separated until the baby spontaneously leaves the breast. The couple can be warmed up with a blanket and the mother can be helped to see her baby by lifting a bit her back with pillows.   Early breastfeeding initiation can save children's life by ensuring long term breastfeeding success. It is also considered a prevention strategy that can help national health care systems saving on expenses.

The advantages of early initiation reach their maximum potential with the Breast Crawl, which seems like the sweetest start for the baby to adjust to the extrauterin environment. It seems to be the way that better boosts the development of babies' nervous system, too.

(Source: www.breastcrawl.org From this website you can find more information and see a real amazing Breast Crawl video)

The Very First Drops…

Importance of colostrum

Colostrum is the very first milk, produced by mammary glands during late pregnancy and immediately after delivery. Its color may vary from white to yellow, orange, pink, green and brown. It is produced in small quantity but it is a concentrate of substances which are crucial for newborns' health. It continues for few days and slowly gives way to breast-milk.

It is extremely rich of antibodies (that is why it has been called "the first vaccination"), vitamin A and factors needed for growth. It has laxative properties to help babies eliminate meconium (first stools).

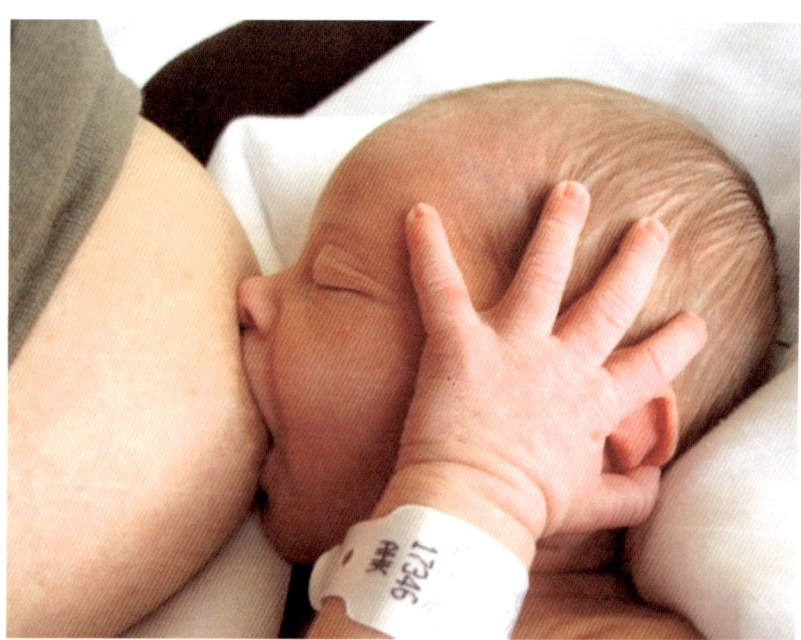

Photo by La Leche League Italia

This prevents a newborn from suffering from jaundice.

It is very important to let the baby have colostrum. The baby must not be separated from his mother after birth and he must be allowed to nurse every time he asks for it. If such conditions are met, no other supplementation is needed.

Even in case of separation due to medical emergencies, the mother should be helped to express her colostrum and give it to her baby.

Birth of Love

Developing a bond with your baby

Dr. William Sears is the father of eight children and one of the most famous American pediatricians. He wrote many beautiful books on child rearing and developed a very insightful way to define the kind of bond that parents may build with their children. What he calls 'attachment parenting' has to do with a sensitive, responsive, intuitive parenting style, when parents are in tune with their children to such an extent that they can recognize their needs, understand their clues and be prone to satisfy them. Attachment parenting has to do with empathy and love. The opposite condition is that of 'detachment parenting', which creates apathy and isolation. Parents and the child seem to walk on parallel channels without finding a real meeting point. It is the result of having one's parenting style based on preconceived notions and external guidelines, rather than on the real relationship and experience with that particular child.

Breastfeeding can help you to develop an attachment style of parenting, because it teaches how to respond to your babies needs, rather than blindly abiding by the dos and don'ts of the doctors, relatives and the other members of the society or following the clock to accomplish external schedules.

As we mentioned in the above chapters, the specific hormonal condition of breastfeeding mothers (high prolactin and oxytocin levels) is by itself a powerful help that nature has given to women in order to tune them up with their babies' needs.

Skin to skin touch (which comes with breastfeeding as well) is another crucial aspect in the initial bonding with our babies. The tiny creature which has just come out in this noisy, unknown, cold world

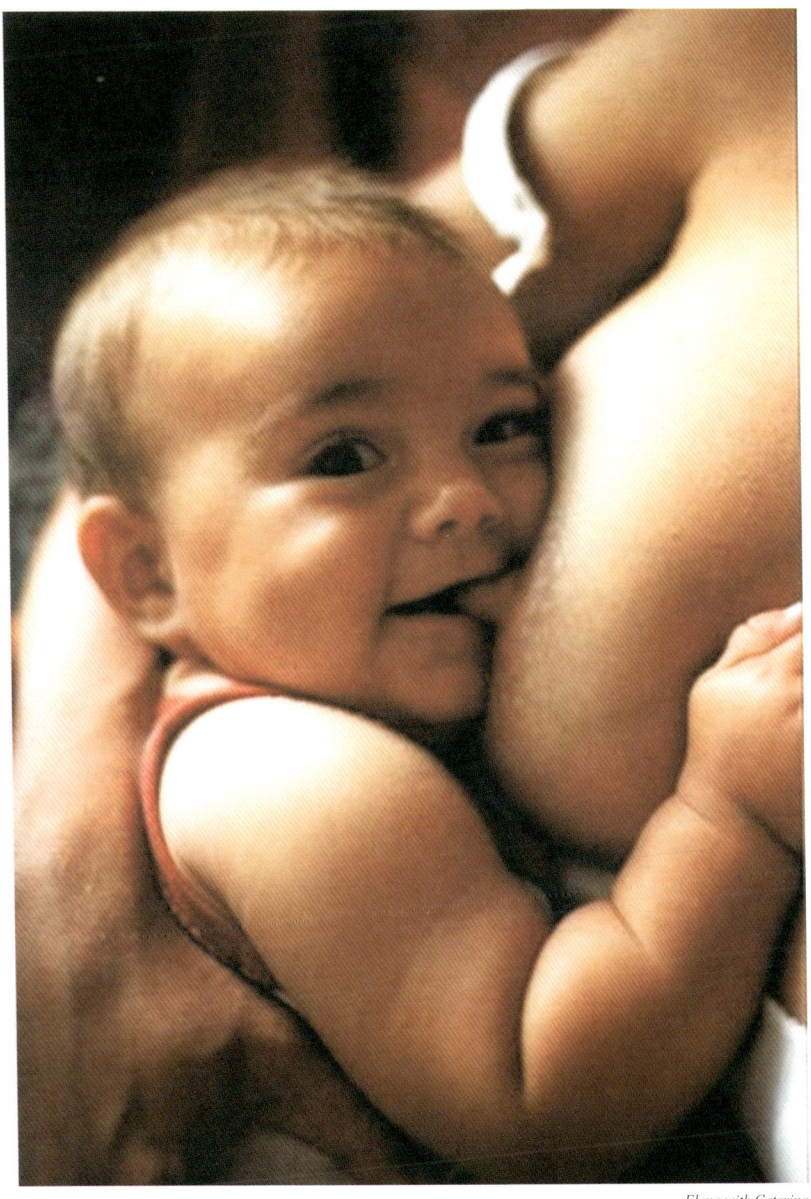

Elena with Caterina

from the protected, peaceful womb where he was constantly caressed by his mother's body and swung by her movements, derives a lot of benefits from touch. Tribal societies keep massaging and touching their babies' bodies and carrying them constantly. It has been noticed that in such societies babies almost never cry! Why? That's because their needs are instantly satisfied. They have constant access to their mother's skin and breast. They are constantly carried and moved as they were in the womb: there is no abrupt separation between life in uterus and outside, everything goes smooth and gradual.

It has been seen that skin to skin touch with mother (preferably direct touch, with no clothes in between) helps a sleepy baby to wake up and a restless one to relax. It also helps the baby to thermoregulate: it warms him up in case he is cold and refreshes him in case he is hot.

There are many ways to 'wear' your baby like tribals do. This gives touch and comfort to the baby and leaves the mother with free hands to do whatever she wants. It has been seen that babies who are carried, sleep longer and better, nurse more frequently and have an overall better growth rate!

It is very important for new parents to assert themselves and build their own parenting style. Relatives, doctors and experts might have the longest experience in child rearing, but ultimately every child is unique and parents should use their intuition rather than blindly follow others' advices. And grandparents and other well-meaning people should learn to respect such intuition and the uniqueness of parent-child relation.

And Here We Start

Importance of a good latching

A good positioning and latching is the first crucial step to successful breastfeeding. It ensures that the baby will get enough milk and that the mother will not experience pain during breastfeeding. If the baby latches correctly, the breast is properly emptied and milk supply will be adequate. The earlier a mother and her baby learn correct latching, the easier everything will follow. Let us see it step by step.

Positioning

First of all the mother should be comfortable, whether she is sitting or lying down, she should not create muscular tensions. Her position should be such that she should be able to breastfeed for long stretches of time. Pillows can be used as supports under the mother's arms, behind her back and under the baby, in order to sustain him at the breast level without tiring the mother's arm. If properly supported the baby feels secure too.

Photo by La Leche League Italia

The baby should be moved towards the breast and not otherwise. The baby's head should bend slightly backwards in order to ease the swallowing. It should not be blocked.

The baby's ear, shoulder and hip should be aligned on a parallel line and the little body should be kept facing towards the mother's body (belly to belly). The baby's nose should be at the nipple level.

The breast can be supported by gently placing a hand underneath, hand palm near your chest and thumb up ('C' hold). The so called 'scissor' or 'cigarette' hold should not be used because it can impede milk flow and create obstructions and engorgements.

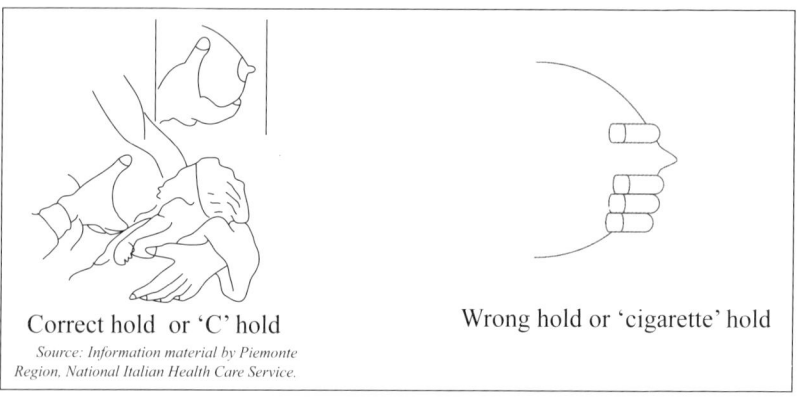

Correct hold or 'C' hold

Wrong hold or 'cigarette' hold

Source: Information material by Piemonte Region, National Italian Health Care Service.

Correct latching

While latching, it is important that the baby's mouth is widely open. This ensures that the baby will not simply grab the nipple, but a good portion of the areola. The mother should wait for his mouth to be open enough, without forcing. In order to have the baby open his mouth, she can repeatedly caress his nose and mouth with her nipple. This will make him search for the breast. Once the mouth is open enough, the baby can be gently moved towards the breast (moving the full arm and without blocking his head).

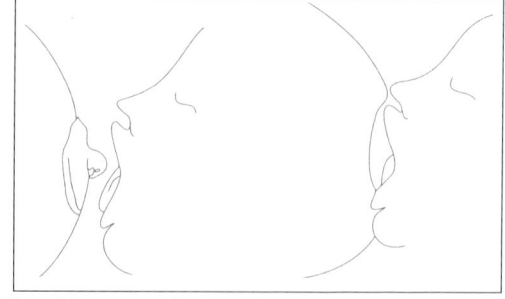

Source: Information material by Piemonte Region, National Italian Health Care Service.

Correct latching is asymmetrical: the first parts to touch the breast are the baby's chin and his/her lower lip. The lower lip and tongue hold a good portion of the areola and the edge of the nipple is far back in the baby's mouth, just up to the junction between the hard and the soft palate.

In this way the baby will hold more of the lower side of the areola than the upper one (how much of it varies according to babies' mouths and different dimensions of nipples and areolas). The baby's chin (not the nose) remains attached to the breast and his lips (especially the lower one) are turned outwards. The baby's inclination should allow him to look at his mother.

If the baby is latched on properly and he is getting milk, the mother will be able to hear him swallow and she will see that he is swallowing

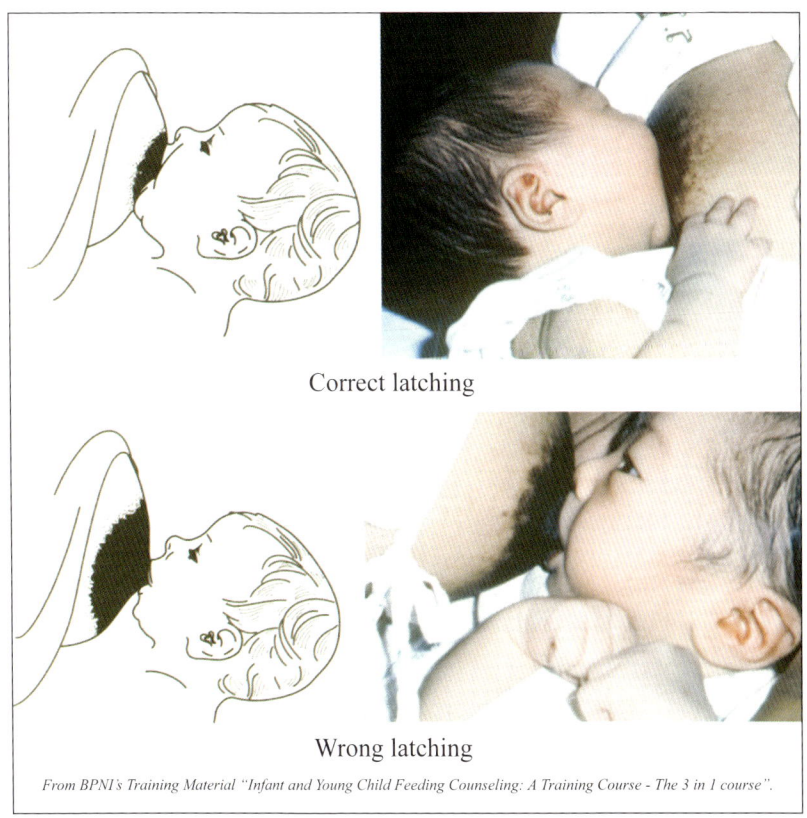

Correct latching

Wrong latching

From BPNI's Training Material "Infant and Young Child Feeding Counseling: A Training Course - The 3 in 1 course".

from the movement of his jaws and facial muscles as well. Suction movements are rapid when the baby starts nursing and they become deep and slow after few minutes, with pauses for swallowing. Few minutes after the baby has started nursing the **let-down reflex** releases milk from all compartments of the breast towards the nipple, through ducts and ductules. This reflex can happen many times in the course of a nursing session and it is stimulated by the release of oxytocin hormone, a consequence of proper stimulation of the breast (For example correct latching). It can be inhibited by stress, use of certain medications, excessive consumption of alcohol and caffeine, hormonal problems. It is crucial to allow the baby get enough milk. Some mothers can tell that let down reflex is happening from physical sensations, like sudden breast fullness or light cramps, some others do not experience any of these. Basically we know that let down is happening by seeing the baby's suction movement become slow and deep, alternated by swallowing.

Artificial nipples and pacifiers should not be given to babies, at least not during the first months, because sucking from those is different from that of sucking from a mother's breast and this can create confusion in a child who is still learning to latch and a suction technique. Furthermore, they reduce the frequency of nursing, which is so crucial to establish a good milk supply.

CHART 7
DIFFERENT SUCTION TECHNIQUES:
BOTTLE AND BREAST.

From these two images you can notice that sucking from a bottle is different from sucking from the breast: the tongue remains inside the gums margin in case of bottle feeding, while it is visible from the baby's mouth in case of breastfeeding. Artificial nipples are not modeled for the baby's mouth like breast nipples and areolas are and they do not reach the junction between hard and soft palate. The baby's mouth is more widely open for breastfeeding.

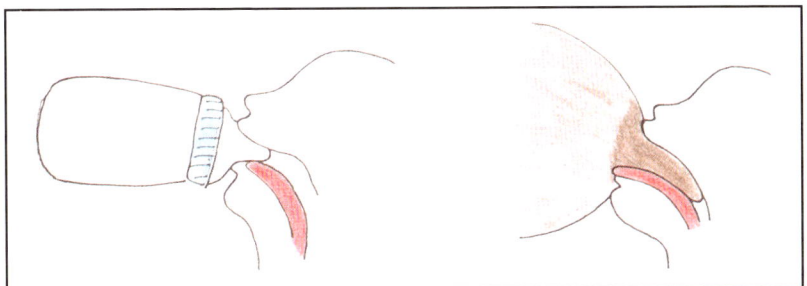

Bottle sucking and Breast sucking

Shape and size do not matter

May they be big or small, the shape or size of breasts has nothing to do with the capacity to produce milk.

Nipples come in different shapes as well. Whatever is the shape and dimension of her nipples, any woman can breastfeed. More or less difficulties can initially be there, according to the interaction between dimension of the nipple and shape of the baby's mouth (For example big nipple / small mouth), but they can all be solved with a bit of patience and help.

Even the so called flat and inverted nipples do not compromise successful breastfeeding.

Inverted nipples are those that sink down into the breast instead of protruding when stimulated (For example, by touching or rubbing them).

In order to see if you have inverted nipples you can gently press with two fingers on both the sides of the areola and see if the nipple comes out or goes back. If it goes back it is an inverted one. This case is not very common though.

Some babies who have a good latch can nurse without problems even in case of inverted nipples (remember that babies 'breastfeed', they do not 'nipple feed'). Others might have some difficulties and a treatment might be needed. A lactation consultant will be able to help you.

In case of flat (those nipples which do not protrude but they do not sink backwards either) are called inverted nipples. It is particularly important not to give the baby any artificial nipples and pacifiers.

Breastfeeding Management

Positions

Here are some positions that you can experiment to breastfeed your baby.

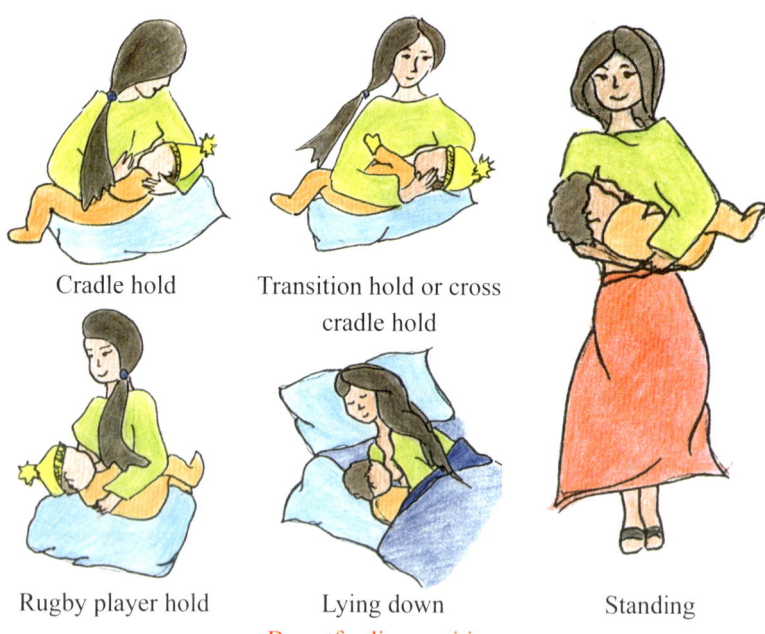

Cradle hold

Transition hold or cross cradle hold

Rugby player hold

Lying down

Standing

Breastfeeding positions

Forget the clock

We are human beings, not machines. And so are our babies. Nursing on demand is the key to adequate milk supply, because breasts are emptied according to babies' needs.

Trying to set babies on fixed nursing schedules proves to be very unproductive. Breasts will not be emptied with the necessary frequency and milk production will drop. Schedules have been made for formula fed infants. Nevertheless this look-at-the-watch method is being questioned even for them! Formula milk never varies in its composition and we know exactly how much milk a bottle fed baby has drunk, because we can see how much is left in a bottle.

This is not applicable to a breastfed baby. We cannot see "how much milk is left in the breast" (not even by expressing it after the nursing session is over) because breasts are not containers to be emptied: they produce milk continuously, even while the child is sucking. And breast milk composition varies continuously even during the same nursing session. Our tiny newborns know perfectly how much they need provided that they are latching well. They will ask for breast milk whenever they need it and their suction pattern will vary according to their hunger and thirst. Breasts will give them exactly what they need at that very moment: watery milk if they are thirsty, fat nutritious one if they are hungry. That is why a correctly breast fed baby who is younger than six months does not need anything else other than mother's milk. Not even water in the hottest weather!

This magic works if there are no external interferences, which means no fixed timings for nursing. Leave the clocks and learn to observe your baby's clues. Some are fast drinkers from the very beginning and can empty one breast in five minutes. Some others might take one hour or more before being satiated.

Be prepared for long, frequent nursing (especially during the night), at least for the first months. Later on your baby might become faster or drink less frequently, but this varies from child to child.

A newborn baby will probably want to nurse every one-two hours. But this is not a mathematical law. Babies are not clocks and their needs vary during day and night. They might nurse very frequently and even continuously during certain moments of the day or night and then be satisfied for many hours. This is a very normal behavior called 'cluster' nursing and it should not be blocked.

We suggest finding comfortable positions to nurse, have a special place with something to read, music, handy healthy snacks and drinks. If you have older children you can keep them close to you, read them a story or preserve special toys just for those special moments and place. You may keep some nutritious snacks for them as well.

During the night you can lie down with your baby (using pillows to be more comfortable, if needed) and try to get some sleep while he nurses. For some women this might be difficult at the beginning, but with a bit of practice it becomes very natural and pleasant.

Even shifting breast according to fixed timings (For example, 15-20 minutes per side) does not make much sense. The best way to go about nursing is letting your baby drink from one breast until he leaves it spontaneously (except specific cases that we will analyze in the following chapters). In this way, you can be sure that he has taken enough nutritious fat milk, which is released only later in the course of nursing.

After finishing one breast you will see if your baby is satiated or he needs more from the other side. If the baby does not need more and your breasts feel uncomfortably full, you can express some milk manually to prevent engorgement.

Growth sprints

Babies periodically go through periods of intense growth generally (though not always) around the second-third and sixth week and around the third month. During such periods (growth sprints or growth spurts) your baby might want to nurse more frequently, maybe almost non-stop. It is normal. He does this in order to increase your milk supply up to his higher need. If you allow him to nurse whenever he wants, soon the supply will meet the demand and the nursing frequency will go back to the normal patterns.

Taking out the nipple from the baby's mouth

If you need to interrupt a nursing session for any reason, do not try to simply pull the nipple out of your baby's mouth, because this will hurt you.

Instead, gently open your baby's mouth by placing a finger between his upper and lower lips, just at the corner of his mouth. Alternatively, you may also pull his chin down softly with one finger. Take the nipple out only once his mouth is open.

Recognizing your baby's hunger signals

Cry is a very late signal of hunger. At that point the baby is desperate. Latching on properly might be difficult and he might not have any patience left to wait for the milk to flow.

A newborn shows that he is hungry through a variety of signals; he might move his jaws and lips the way he does for sucking, or search around with his mouth, suck his hands or the blanket. It is important to learn to recognize babies' hunger signals and nurse them before this hunger becomes unbearable for them.

The first weeks

During the first weeks of breastfeeding babies and mothers learn the art of nursing. It is a crucial period of mutual knowledge, when lots of patience and good will is required. Some babies go smooth about nursing. Some others may require a little more help, according to specific circumstances. It is very important to hold on during these first, often tiring days. Tiredness will soon be paid back by immense satisfaction, even in the most difficult cases. Concentrate on learning to latch, avoid pacifiers, artificial nipples and any other food than your milk. In the next chapters you will find alternative methods to supplement (in case a real need arises) and we will teach you how to evaluate your baby's growth. Hold on and do not hesitate to ask for help! It is worth the effort.

During this period the milk might leak from your breasts. It is normal; your breasts are learning to adjust the milk supply to your baby's demand. Soon this will stop because they will produce only the needed quantity of milk. Meanwhile you can wear cotton pads under your bra, to avoid having your clothes wet. There are specific disposable pads available in the market; if you opt for this solution try to prefer perspiring varieties (For example, not covered with plastic) and keep changing them very frequently. If nipples remain humid they might get hurt more easily and healing eventual cracks will take longer.

Optimal duration of breastfeeding

The World Health Organization (WHO) recommends exclusive breastfeeding for at least six months from birth and breastfeeding accompanied by appropriate complementary foods for at least two years. There is no indication on when to stop, after the second year is completed. Breastfeeding should be prolonged according to the need and comfort of each— baby and the mother.

CHART 8
DID YOU KNOW?

Mother's milk has several healing properties— helps a stuffy nose to open up, helps healing conjunctivitis if put in the affected eye, a cloth dipped in mother's milk if placed between a nappy and the baby's skin heals nappy rashes. Again, a few drops spread on the nipple after nursing prevents and heals nipple pain better than any industrial lotion or oil.

(Source: Tiziana Catanzani, Paola Negri, Allattare un gesto d'amore, Bonomi, 2005, p. 24)

Every Baby is Unique

Children have different styles, personalities and constitution right from the time they are born. These show even in the way the approach the breast and in their nursing patterns.

Some are very eager to nurse and will take time to suck with calm. Some others drink fast and empty the breast in few minutes. It is quite probable that these last ones will swallow air while drinking and hence suffer from colic pains. They might want to nurse more frequently for shorter periods of time. In this case it is better to check whether the baby is getting enough milk, by counting wet nappies, like we will explain in the next chapter.

There are also sleepy babies who tend to sleep for long stretches of time and fall asleep after few minutes of nursing. Apparently they are very peaceful babies but the fact is that it is a dangerous condition. Since they do not nurse frequently and they sleep instead of actively sucking, they might not be getting enough milk. Note that many babies fall asleep while nursing, which is fine. We are here talking of those children who fall asleep almost as soon as they start sucking. Sometimes they are just a week old or maybe because of low weight at birth, and the problem will be solved as they grow little stronger. Sometimes they are drowsy because of medications given to their mother during delivery (cesarean section, epidural anesthesia, etc.) or because they need to recover from a difficult birth experience (operative deliveries). They need to be encouraged to nurse frequently and to be kept alert while they suck, by touching their feet or stimulating their suction by gently rubbing a finger on their chicks, just at the level of their lips junction. A very effective technique to keep them awake is shifting breast every few minutes, as soon as the baby seems about to fall asleep. You may try to change the baby's nappy in between a nursing session or to take out the breast from his mouth when he falls asleep and keep him in a vertical positions for a minute. This sometimes wakes them up.

Some children get distracted at the minimum noise and need a very quiet environment, free from stimulations, in order to nurse properly. Many go through such a phase around the fourth to the sixth month, when they start discovering the world.

Some children seem to throw out everything they drink: they might simply regurgitate frequently or they might vomit. They may suffer from reflux, which is a condition that normally disappears when the child grows a little bigger. We will discuss this problem in detail.

There are babies who seem to be really fussy about everything. They seem to be never satisfied, never at ease. Dr. Sears calls them 'high need' babies. It is a very positive way to look at the problem: they simply need more of us. Sometimes their dissatisfaction derives from physical discomfort (For example, reflux or colic pain). Sometimes, Dr. Sears says, 'they simply miss the womb'. I find this expression very insightful. Children come to this world after spending nine months in the protected softness of the uterus, where they are constantly touched in touch with the mothers' body, and calmed by the familiar rhythm of her heartbeat. For some of them this big change is not such a problem, but for some others it is. They need reassurance; lots of touch, being held and carried, being allowed to keep their head on their mothers' chest, so that they can feel her heart beating. In this way their puzzled experience is recomposed. Well, this works magically! They get adapted soon and thrive well.

Photo by Roberta Roberto.

Babies' Growth

Babies grow at different speeds and with different rhythms. Even rural women know that some babies have a rapid growth during the first months and years of their life, while some others grow later, maybe during adolescence. Nowadays, we seem to have forgotten that babies always grew well even when scales and percentile curves did not exist and we literally freak out if we see our neighbor's child growing faster than ours. We are so obsessed by this dimension issue that we have come to the point that we confuse 'healthy' with 'big' and sometimes with 'fat'! On the contrary, health is a complex multidimensional concept, which includes much more than our babies' weight and height and head circumference. These are just some (and not even the most important) of the parameters to evaluate our children's health status. Nevertheless the first thing that most pediatricians do is place a baby on a scale.

Here we will give few indications on how to evaluate a babies' growth, keeping in mind that they are not absolute musts. If our baby is getting enough milk (see the next paragraph) and his health status is overall good (he is happy, playful and responds to stimulations in a way which is appropriate to his age small variations from the norm are absolutely no reason for worrying.

Let us also keep in mind that babies grow according to their genetic potential. Small or thin parents cannot expect their baby to be excessively tall and big.

Method to know if your child is getting enough milk

Count his dirty nappies. A child who is getting enough milk will wet (we mean nicely wet) at least 4-5 disposable nappies or 6-8 cloth nappies within 24 hours and he will defecate at least 1-2 times during the same stretch of time.

Normal growth parameters

During the first 3-4 days of life it is normal for the baby to lose weight – up to 5-7 % of the birth weight. A loss up to 10% is still considered acceptable but it is a sign that the mother needs help with the management of breastfeeding. If breastfeeding proceeds normally babies should recover their birth weight by their tenth or the fifteenth day of life. If this does not happen, then the mother should consider asking competent help from a breastfeeding expert.

Weight gain should not be calculated from birth weight but from the lowest weight reached, three-four days after delivery.

During the first three-four months of life, babies should normally gain 120-200 grams per week (approximately 500 grams per month). Breastfed children often grow faster than bottle-fed children during the first weeks and later on they might grow slower. It is normal so no need to worry. During the second trimester breastfed children might slow down their growth rhythm. A minimum of 80 grams per week is normal (approximately 300-350 grams per month). Do not panic if there are months when your child does not gain weight at all! It can happen and it can be normal, as long as the child is not *loosing* weight. It should be an alarm bell to monitor your breastfeeding management and keep track of all the other health parameters (sometimes even just a flu in the family has a temporary impact on babies' growth) but it does not necessarily mean that something is going wrong.

After breastfeeding is established, checking your child's weight every week does not make any sense. Once a month is more than enough.

Checking your baby's weight before and after feeding is absolutely useless. As we know, milk varies in its composition every moment of the day and during the same nursing session. A child who is being nursed on demand will get enough nutrients through the whole day and night, but the total amount of such nutrients will not be equally distributed among the various nursing sessions. Furthermore, he will take more or less milk according to the need of the moment. As you can see, knowing how much milk a child has exactly drunk each and every time he nurses, is of no use.

Remember that growth parameters may be the 'norm', but deviations from the norm do not always mean lack of health or breastfeeding problems. There are babies who grow faster than others. Exclusively, breastfed children will not grow obese and there is no need to put them 'on a diet'. Keep feeding them on demand. Obesity is a condition that will eventually appear later in life if complementary nutrition will not be based on healthy foods. It has nothing to do with the frequency of breastfeeding. Breastfeeding is indeed a protective factor against obesity.

Other babies grow very slow. This is an alarm bell to check if they are getting enough milk and perhaps seek for competent help, to be sure we are managing breastfeeding correctly. It may be appropriate to monitor their overall health status. But if everything is fine, the baby is healthy, he wets and dirties enough nappies, he latches on properly and he is fed on demand, then there is no need to worry. Simply, that baby's growth rhythm is slow. That is fine.

Percentiles, percentiles...

Sadly percentile growth charts were initially built on formula fed children's growth standards. And for breastfed children, growth has been evaluated according to those parameters.

Even more sadly, many doctors keep evaluating breastfed children's growth using those standards, even now that new charts have been made by the WHO specifically for the breastfed children.

It is very likely that the growth of a breastfed baby will appear to be poor, if evaluated using parameters which are based on formula feeding. As we mentioned above, growth patterns are different in the two cases! Before panicking, it is important to know what charts our pediatrician is using to monitor our children's growth. And we shall be ready to discuss the matter with him.

Remember that percentile curves have been made on *healthy* children on a huge population of healthy children. Even if your child suppose is on the 2nd percentile, this means that 2% of the whole populations of healthy babies used to build those standards is smaller than or as big as him. And this 2% actually means *hundreds* of children!

When the baby is not getting enough milk...

Sometimes babies are really not getting enough milk. The real signs of your baby not getting enough milk are inadequate or low weight gain, less then six-eight wet disposable diapers (four-five cloth nappies) within 24 hours, less than one bowel movement within 24 hours. Another sign (though not very reliable) might be that the mother does not feel relief in her breasts fullness after feeding. She may also not hear the baby swallowing while he nurses.

These circumstances require adjustment in the breastfeeding technique. We suggest seeking the support of a breastfeeding expert, like a lactation consultant, and at the same time try to work in collaboration with the pediatrician to monitor the overall health status of your baby. Remember that more suckling makes more milk and if you are confident, milk will flow in plenty.

Other reasons of low milk supply could be the use of estrogens and sometimes progesterone, fertility medications, breast surgery, drugs, retained placenta (For example, when pieces of placenta remain in the uterus instead of being expelled after delivery; but this is uncommon).

There are mothers who are really incapable to produce enough milk, but this condition is *extremely rare*. In any case even a bit of mother milk is better than nothing and even women who cannot produce *enough* milk can and should breastfeed with the aid of appropriate supplementation devices.

Improving your breastfeeding technique

First of all you should consider (with competent help) if your baby is latching properly. Sore nipples are in most cases a sign of wrong latching. When latching is not the problem, you may consider the frequency and duration of nursing asking yourself how often does my child nurse? For how long is he feeding? Do you feed him every time he asks for it or are you trying to set him on a schedule?

Feed him every time he wants. Try to encourage a sleepy child to nurse more frequently (at least every two hours, also during the night) and keep him alert while he nurses. You may try to shift breasts frequently. In this way the child will also get more milk from repeated let-down reflexes.

Breast compression

Breast compression is a technique that helps the baby to get more milk and it should be used when he is sucking but not actively drinking. In this, the mother holds her breast with one hand, thumb on the upper side and rest of the fingers on the lower side (keeping her hand as backwards towards the chest as possible). When the baby starts suckling she compresses her breast gently but firmly (don't worry, this will NOT increase the risk of obstructed ducts). Milk will flow down to the nipple and will keep the baby drinking.

If the technique does not seem to work after few tentative, the mother might try to shift breast and repeat the experiment. The technique works better at the beginning of a nursing session when the milk flow is faster.

Herbal remedies

Keeping in mind that these are not the solution of breastfeeding problems but just a complementary help, in every region of the world there are herbs which are traditionally considered helpful to increase the milk supply. The most common are cumin, anise seeds, fennel, fenugreek, raspberry leaf, borage, goat's rue (*Galega Opphicinalis*). Try to discover what herbs are available in your region. What were your 'granny's remedies' and drink infusions; if nothing else happens, they will hydrate you and relax you!

Note that 'drinking milk or consuming dairies in order to produce milk' is only a myth and it might cause allergies or intolerances.

Domperidone

Again, not the remedy but just a complementary help, the very experienced breastfeeding consultant Jack Newman suggests the use of Domperidone in order to increase the milk supply. This should be done only in specific circumstances (consult a breastfeeding specialist) and under medical supervision.

Alternative supplementation techniques

There are cases in which a baby may need temporary supplementation. This does not necessary mean formula. Sometimes expressed mother milk or colostrum is enough. If not, then the first choice should be donated human milk, if a milk bank is present in your area. Only if this option is also not available, one should opt for formulas.

However the milk is supplemented, it is important to avoid bottles and artificial nipples, because they will create confusion in the baby's suction technique and most likely they will make the breastfeeding problem, worse. The idea is to help the child improve his suction technique and gradually wean off the supplementation. You may ask the help of a breastfeeding expert regarding this matter. The same person can help you choose which supplementing technique works best for you and your child and she or he will teach you how to use it properly.

Alternative methods to give supplements

Lactation aid

It can be bought ready made or made at home with a few simple materials; a syringe without needle (30 or 60 ml) or a glass/cup or a bottle (to be filled with milk), a pipe of small diameter, which should be long enough to reach the breast level easily (it can be found in shops selling medical equipment).

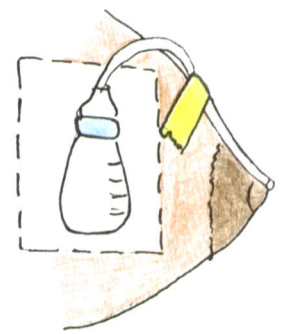

One side of the pipe goes in place of the needle on the syringe (or inside the bottle/cup/glass), the other goes at the level of the nipple (it can be held by the mother's hand or fixed on the breast with tape) and in the baby's mouth (use two pipes in case of twins). The container should be placed at the level of the breast, just slightly higher than the baby's head. You may tie the container to your neck with a band. It is better to direct the pipe towards the baby's palate so that it remains still. You may decide to use the aid as you start nursing or after some time. When the baby sucks from the breast, the milk flows from the container into his mouth.

You should be able to see the milk flow through the pipe and your baby swallow with periodic pauses during the swallowing. If this does not happen, it means that something is not working right.

You will need to clean containers and pipes with care. Pipes are very small but it is important to remove any trace of milk with hot water, every time you use them. You cannot boil them because they would melt, but you can repeatedly have water flowing through until they are clean. They must be changed every week.

This method is very good because it allows mother and baby to learn breastfeeding and provides the baby the comfort of being touched and held which comes with breastfeeding. If you use this method it is less likely that the baby, getting use to supplementations, refuses the breast of his mother.

Finger feeding

It is useful in case the baby refuses the breast or if breastfeeding has to be temporary interrupted for exceptional reasons.

You need a syringe or a container and a tiny pipe, as for the lactation aid. You can again tie the container to your neck or place it on a table near you. One end of the pipe goes into the container and the other has to be fixed to your finger. Your nails must be short and your hands very clean. Make sure that the edge of the pipe does not go beyond your finger's top digit.

Hold your baby in a normal *cradle hold* or *rugby player* position, taking care that his head is slightly lifted up.

Gently stimulate your child to open his mouth, by caressing it with your finger. Then introduce the finger in his mouth (with the digit towards the palate). While the baby is sucking, move your finger's tip gently and gradually towards the junction point of his hard palate and the soft palate.

You should be able to see your baby swallow the milk flowing through the pipe with periodic pauses during the swallowing. If this does not happen, it means that something is not working right.

In case the baby curls his tongue, gently caress it to straighten it. This is a simple exercise that you can do even while you are not feeding him, to help him learn how to straighten his tongue. It is more effective if you do this while holding your baby with his tummy on your knees.

Particularly weak babies might need two pipes instead of one, to obtain a decent milk flow. The device must be cleaned with care like the lactation aid.

Cup, syringe or dropper, spoon

These are also very old and valid supplementation techniques. Whatever instrument you chose, you should carefully hold your baby with his head up and let very few drops of milk flow into his mouth at one time. Never force the baby. Never *push* the milk down in his mouth. Let the baby explore with his mouth, lick the milk and be sure he is interested in going on. If he is, proceed *slowly*.

Common Problems and Their Treatments

Baby's problems

Colic pain

It is a very common problem, since the newborn's digestive system is still immature and when he swallows air it might create fermentation in his intestines creating a lot of pain. The same problem can have different degrees of severity; from mild, isolated episodes, to repeated, acute ones (often happening approximately everyday at the same time). The baby cries inconsolably, his belly becomes hard; he straightens his legs and passes gas. These episodes are often followed by greenish, foamy feces. It is a phenomenon which happens little more frequently in fast drinkers. It normally disappears after the third month, when the baby's digestive system becomes more mature.

There is no final cure to this problem but we can try a few remedial measures:

- Try to eliminate the cause; sometimes colic pains are due to alimentary allergies or intolerances to some foods in the mother's diet. Try to eliminate the suspected foods (starting with dairy products), observe the reaction and eventually modify your diet (see: *Mother's nutrition*).
- Give your baby regular massage on his tummy (gentle but firm), *before* he is actually in pain.

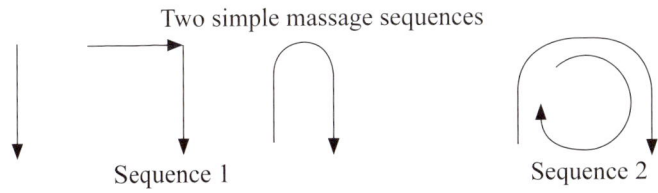

Two simple massage sequences

Sequence 1   Sequence 2

- During the crisis, hold your baby in a position that will keep his abdomen compressed (For example, with his tummy on your arm or on your knees).

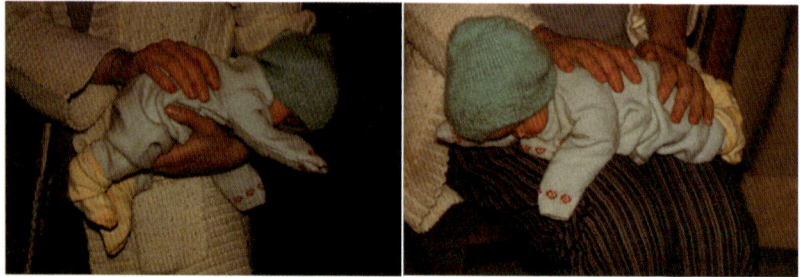

Reflux

Babies' stomach is immature too and during the first months it might be slightly opened on the upper side, which can cause milk to be thrown up. In some cases this is accompanied by frequent regurgitation or vomit. In some others nothing comes out of the baby's mouth but the milk goes up and down inside and this causes pain. The baby might suddenly cry inconsolably with no other apparent reason or just be dissatisfied or unhappy between one nursing and the next. He might salivate abundantly or keep making swallowing movement and/or disgusted expressions. Again, this problem normally resolves after the third month.

Remember that vomiting, especially regurgitating are not always symptoms of reflux. These are normal self regulating systems which allow the baby to throw out what he has taken in excess. A baby's vomiting can be very violent. It can be thrown even at a meter distance. Parents sometimes are scared by this; but it is normal. Throwing the vomit so far is a protection from choking.

Breastfeeding should be continued. No formula (not even those specially designed for reflux!) is easier to digest and absorb than mother's milk!

In order to ease the pain and limit the problem you can keep the child with his head and stomach raised while you feed him and afterwards. For this purpose you may carry him or feed him in a sling.

Try to not over feed him in one nursing session. Nurse him more frequently, but in less quantity. You may give him just one breast at a time. Severe cases might need antacid medications and sometimes operation (in rare cases). This has to be evaluated by your doctor.

Babies refusing the breast
Some babies refuse the breast because they feel uncomfortable. This requires an adjustment in the positioning. Sometimes they prefer one breast over the other because of anatomic differences between the two sides or differences in the way the mother holds them. Sometimes this different liking is due to temporary problems, like ear infection from one side or one of the nostrils being blocked. You can check and try to understand the reason of your baby's discomfort. Sometimes the same uneasiness can be due to muscular contractions caused by delivery. These might resolve spontaneously or need the help of an osteopath or an orthopedic.

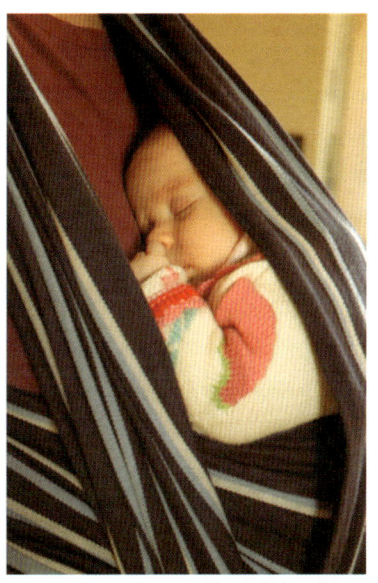

Photo by Roberta Roberto

Some babies might be disturbed by a very powerful let-down reflex or abundant flow. You can try to express some milk before nursing the baby, so that the flow will be slower. Your baby might like to nurse lying prone on your stomach, so that the gravity force will keep milk flow under control.

Babies on a strike
It can happen that a baby suddenly refuses the breast for some days, when he is not yet ready for solids or in any case not ready for weaning.

He might refuse to nurse totally or accept it only during certain moments (For example, in the night).

It does not mean that the baby is suddenly weaning himself. Weaning is a gradual process and it does not happen like this. Normally the reason behind such behavior is a condition of stress related to nursing and to the general family life. It may happen that the mother is busy and she has not been feeding the baby on demand, or maybe some major event happening (for example, shifting house) is keeping everyone busy and preoccupied. The mother should be patient, dedicate quality time to her baby, keep inviting him to nurse without forcing. Everything will go back to normal within a few days. Meanwhile she should express her milk with the frequency her baby was drinking before the 'strike', in order to prevent engorgements and maintain a high milk supply.

The biter

When a baby tends to bite the nipple (this often happens while teething, when children try to bite everything to ease their gums discomfort) the best way to discourage him is gently pushing his face against the breast and firmly saying 'no'. The baby will instantly open his mouth to breath and he will leave the nipple. The same effect can be obtained by gently closing his nose with your fingers. Shouting at the baby can scare him and discourage him from nursing at all. Pushing him away can hurt you even more; if the baby closes his jaws tight on the nipple. Many biters can be actually stopped before the mischief takes place, as mothers normally become good at understanding that their baby is going to bite, just by looking at his facial expression. You may give your baby something else to bite before restarting nursing.

Mother's problems

Sore nipples and cracks

During the first weeks, the mother might have pain in her nipples or even real cracks. The cause is normally bad or poor latching. For breastfeeding to continue, mother and baby must improve and correct their latching technique. This is the only real and effective cure.

The baby should be fed on demand. When he is not yet excessively hungry, otherwise his ability to latch properly will be compromised by his impatience due to desperation.

Here are some *palliative* remedies to ease the pain and facilitate healing (remember that they are not *the cure* for the problem):

- After feeding, spread some mother milk on the nipple and let it dry in the air.
- Let the nipple get as much air as possible. You can be without a bra, or keep the nipple aerated by placing a common kitchen strainer (after removing the handle) between bra and nipple.
- You do not need disinfectants; normal daily hygiene with neutral pH soap is fine. Do not wash your nipples after each nursing!
- Local warm water applications might be helpful to calm the pain.
- Do not apply medicated or any other creams.
- Nipple shields can be a *temporary* help in case the pain is so high that breastfeeding becomes unbearable. Remember that this is not a cure for nipple problems and one should work on the latching and slowly stop using the shield.

Do not use commercial lotions that need to be removed before feeding the baby (residuals might remain on your skin and all this excessive washing might aggravate the problem). 100% purified lanoline is effective and does not need to be removed.

Remember that trying to resist the pain is counterproductive. Waiting aggravates the problem. You should immediately seek for help to find a solution.

If pain persists after ensuring correct latching, this means that the cause is another. Other common causes of nipple pain are:

Fungal infections

The fungus Candida Albicans is normally present in our bacterial flora and it can grow out of proportion given particular circumstances, like: excessive stress and tiredness, excessive consumption of refined foods and sugars, antibiotic therapy, use of synthetic clothes and synthetic nipple pads, vaginal infection before delivery (in this case the baby may contract the fungal infection during delivery and then pass it to the mother). *Symptoms* of fungal infection can be redness and inflammation of the nipple. Sometimes the nipple may appear pink and lucid. Cuts (which do not disappear with normal treatment), bubbles, scaled skin, deep pain (sometimes up to mother's chest and underarm) which do not disappear while the child is not sucking may become a cause of concern for the mother. You may notice white stains inside the baby's mouth. Both mother's nipples and baby's mouth should be treated with appropriate antifungal medicine (normally fluconazole), for at least once in 15 days until the pain disappears. Ask your doctor for treatment and advice. Expose the area to air and sunlight as much as you can. Carefully boil every toy the child puts in his mouth, change his nappy frequently and treat, if needed, baby's genital areas and/or yours and your partner's.

Eczema or allergies

This problem is particularly frequent when the child has started eating solid foods. If some food parts are left in his mouth when he nurses, this may irritate your nipples. Take care of cleaning the child's mouth before nursing him. Sometimes allergic reactions can be due to the use of certain cosmetics, cloth detergents, and synthetic clothes. You should individuate the cause and remove it. Symptoms of eczema and allergies can be red, scaled skin with flat bubbles which tend to scale if touched, itching or burning sensation which persists after nursing.

Herpes

Symptoms of herpes infection are deeply burning watery bubbles with regular shape (similar to those of chickenpox). They burst and turn into cuts and later they form a crust. Diagnosis of herpes can be confirmed in a laboratory by culturing the lesions. If the mother is affected by herpes in areas of the breast which are far from the nipple, she can continue breastfeeding, taking care of covering the affected parts while nursing, to avoid contact with the baby. In case the nipple or very proximate areas are affected, she should temporary suspend breastfeeding from that side or both sides if both nipples are affected. Meanwhile she should keep expressing and throwing her milk, in order to maintain the supply and to be able to restart breastfeeding after healing. Ask your doctor for appropriate antiviral cure. Follow all possible hygienic precaution to avoid baby's contact with affected areas and always wash your hands after touching. Contracting herpes can be very dangerous for babies below three-four weeks of age but there is no danger afterwards.

Obstructed ducts and engorgement

Symptoms are pain or itching sensation in one or more areas of the breast, which are usually hard and swollen. There can be localized redness and heat. Sometimes the areola and the portion of the breast around it can be very hard and swollen which makes latching very difficult for the baby. In this case, you may also find useful to express some drops of milk before starting breastfeeding. This will ease the latching.

Breast engorgement and duct obstruction can be prevented by good latching and frequent feeding. Be sure that your baby is latching properly. If not, correct the latching. If the baby is not latching properly, it means that he is not being able to effectively empty the breasts.

Rest as much as you can with your baby close to you and feed him very often (every hour if required), changing the position frequently. You may try the 'mother wolf' position.

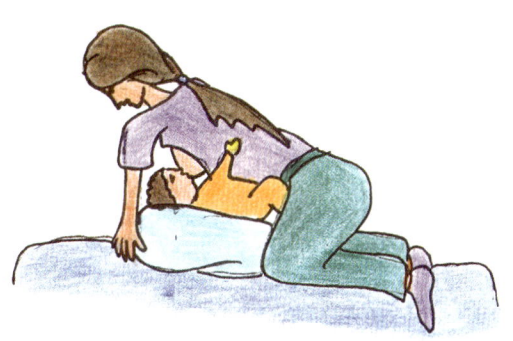

Mother-wolf position

Here the force of gravity helps the milk to flow down. Warm baths and showers or warm water applications right before nursing will help the milk flow. Even slow circular massages all around the breast (from the upper portion towards the nipple) will be helpful at this purpose.

Between one nursing and the other you can ease the inflammation with cold water applications or frozen cabbage leaves to be inserted between breast and bra (after making a hole for the nipple). Keep changing them as they get 'cooked'.

If the areola is too sore and hard, try to express some drops of milk before feeding the baby, in order to ease the latching.

Expressing milk does not help by itself in case of engorgement. Your baby's suction is much more effective in emptying your breasts. Nevertheless it can be useful in case the baby refuses or cannot nurse.

Mastitis (breast infection)

Mastitis occurs with the similar symptoms as breast engorgements, accompanied by fever (higher than 38°C) for more than 24 hours. Even the treatment is the same as for engorged breasts, accompanied by appropriate antibiotic therapy. The mother will need a lot of rest with her baby. The infection does not pass to the baby. Breastfeeding must not be interrupted.

It is very important to cure breast engorgements and infections carefully. If the symptoms aggravate, they can turn into *mammary abscess* which will need medical intervention. Remember that even in such unfortunate circumstance you can continue breastfeeding. Seek competent breastfeeding support if this problem arises.

Vasospasm

It consists of a deep pain in the breast accompanied by whitening of the edge of the nipple. It is due to excessive compression of breast muscles and interruption of blood circulation, normally because the baby's mouth compresses the nipple area too strongly. It is very often connected to poor latching technique. First of all verify how your baby is latched and correct the eventual problems. After this is done, you can try other tricks, like feeding your baby while you make him sit straight (this normally helps him to keep his mouth open) or gently pressing his chin down with a finger as he starts compressing the nipple too much. Some pharmacologic treatments can also relieve the pain (normally nifedipine). Since the problem increases with cold, nursing in a heated environment and warm water applications can be helpful too.

There is a disease called *Raynaud syndrome* whose symptoms are similar to those of vasospasm. It can involve the breasts and other body extremities and it might have appeared already during pregnancy or before. Treatment is the same as above but improvements might be less or slower.

Mother's Nutrition

It is very important for the breastfeeding mother to eat healthy, nutritious food in order to remain positive and not exhaust herself. It is not true that during breastfeeding (neither during pregnancy) you must *eat for two*. On the contrary, you must *nourish two people*. This is a different concept altogether. It means that you need to have a balanced diet, consuming a wide variety of healthy foods in the right proportion and not in excess. For a mother who is neither underweight neither overweight, 500 calories (per day) more than normal are enough.

Avoid junks, refined sugars, fried foods and choose seasonal fresh fruits and vegetables as they are rich in iron, minerals and vitamins, especially those rich in vitamin C, complex carbohydrates (whole cereals, again rich in iron and other minerals), proteins (pulses, non fat meats, fish, eggs), good fats (unrefined local varieties of vegetable oil; butter and clarified butter should be consumed raw, in very moderate quantity. Avoid margarines, hydrogenated fats and trans fats).

Dairies (for example, milk products) are a good source of calcium but they can cause colic pain in some children who cannot digest cow milk proteins. If your child seems to be sensitive to dairies you can try to eliminate them and see the effects. Same is the case with other *potentially allergenic foods* (*for example,* nuts, eggs, fish, citrus fruits, chocolate, soy, tomatoes, potatoes, peppers, eggplant, strawberries, and caffeine). Suspend the suspected food if your child shows symptoms of alimentary allergy or intolerance (irritability, stuffy nose, recurrent colds, restlessness during or after breastfeeding, sudden burning sensation during or after breastfeeding, inconsolable long crying not related to other causes, sleeping problems, sudden awakening with evident discomfort, green feces with mucus, eczema, dermatitis and other skin problems). After staying for *fifteen days* without consuming that particular food eliminate it *totally* and always read food labels to know 'hidden' ingredients. Observe your child; if you notice an improvement, reintroduce that food though in decent quantity. If symptoms reappear, the allergy/intolerance is proven. You should eliminate it from your diet and introduce it in your child's diet as late as you can. If no symptoms reappear, you can restart consuming that food without worrying.

It is true that the taste of mother's milk changes according to what the mother eats, but this is not a reason to avoid particular foods straight away. Babies already know those tastes since the time they were in uterus (through the amniotic fluid) and exposing them to even strong tastes (like cabbage, onions, garlic, etc.) through breast milk reinforces this habit. They mostly do not seem to dislike such tastes and they will be more eager to accept them when solids are introduced.

Getting Rest

Getting rest is very important for breastfeeding mothers, especially during the first months after delivery. Otherwise you might exhaust yourself and compromise your breastfeeding experience, beside risking syndromes like postpartum depression. Leave house-hold chores aside and spend time with your baby. Learn the language of love; all the rest can wait.

Since babies tend to wake up frequently during the night, it is very important that you rest and take naps during the day, when your baby sleeps. For a while, you should tune your own rhythms to your baby's rhythms. Do not expect your baby to sleep through the night, at least not during the first months of his life. But this might not happen at all for few years. It is normal for little babies to wake up frequently to nurse. They need this to keep milk supply high. Given a few exceptions, babies who sleep well through the night are those to worry about, since they might not be taking enough milk. If they sleep for more than

Photo by La Leche League Italia

four-six hours consecutively (and this is already a lot) they should be encouraged to wake up and nurse more often. Frequent nursing is the norm; it is not symptom of milk scarcity! If your baby tends to be sleepy and he is not gaining enough weight, you should encourage him to drink at least every two hours.

Dr. William Sears points out how frequent night waking could be a protective mechanism against crib deaths or SIDS (Sudden Infant Death Syndrome). This seems to happen more frequently to babies who sleep through the night, because they might not have the capacity to wake up in case of breathing interruptions. Irregular breathing and short moments of apnea are otherwise a common phenomenon in small babies whose respiratory system is not yet mature. Sleeping with their mother help babies to tune their breathing rhythm with hers and again prevents SIDS (mother proximity keeps her aware of her child and it is itself another protective factor). Co-sleeping (for example, sleeping with parents) is the norm in most traditional societies (and so it was everywhere up to one century ago). It is the most natural way for the baby and it has many advantages for the mother as well.

Babies' sleeping patterns are different than an adult's. They go through more phases of light sleep (REM phase). This is important for the rapid growth of their brain. It has been proven that when mother and baby sleep together their sleeping phases become coordinated. When the baby is going through a phase of light sleep, so is the mother. It is very common for mothers who share their sleep with their baby to wake up just few seconds before him. It is not a coincidence! This will make night waking less difficult for the mother as it is less tiring to wake up during a phase of light sleep. She will be ready to nurse and probably the let-down reflex will be activated more quickly. The baby will promptly get milk and calm down immediately.

Now see the difference. A baby wakes up alone in a dark room; he does not find anyone and starts crying. The mother will hear him when he is desperate. She will be suddenly woken up from a phase of deep sleep. She will rush to the other room and pick up the desperate baby, who is now too impatient to wait for the milk flow to happen or even to latch correctly. Sleeping with your baby also gives you the possibility to sleep or at least rest while he is nursing.

Breastfeeding and Contraception

Lactation Amenorrhea Method (LAM)
Breastfeeding has a protecting effect (98% safe) against new pregnancies, provided:

- Your baby is younger than six months
- Your periods have not yet restarted
- Your baby is not given any other food or drink than mother milk, neither pacifiers
- Your baby is nursed on demand, with intervals not longer than four hours during the day and not longer than six hours during the night.

Other contraceptive methods
Other contraceptive methods compatible with breastfeeding are barrier methods (condoms, diaphragms), IUD (Intra Uterine Device) and progesterone only oral pills. In some rare cases progesterone might reduce the milk supply, but this has to be evaluated looking through each case at a time and one can always step back on noticing milk scarcity.

Breastfeeding could be used as introductory contraception and later joined by other methods.

Breastfeeding and Physical Acivity

You can practice moderate physical activity during breastfeeding, having care to not exhaust yourself. It is healthy and it can help you reduce the weight accumulated during pregnancy. Remember though that breastfeeding itself serves this purpose beautifully: pregnancy weight gain is in fact meant to be a provision for breastfeeding, which will help you to gradually go back to your normal shape (provided that you avoid junks and you do not overeat)

Milk Expression

When it is needed
- To relief the tension of a very full breast; empty the breast until you fill relieved but not more than that. The more you empty your breasts the more they get filled again.
- To maintain the milk supply in case of temporary interruption of breastfeeding, you should express your milk with the frequency your baby was nursing before the interruption.
- To increase milk supply when the baby's suction is week or for any reason he does not nurse enough frequently emptying the breasts frequently is crucial in order to establish good milk production, especially during the first weeks after delivery or to build a milk supply in case of a delayed start of breastfeeding. In this case you should express your milk at least every two hours for 15-20 minutes.
- To create a reserve of mother's milk in case the mother has to be separated from her baby (for work or other reasons) and to maintain the supply/avoid engorgements.

When it is not needed
- To empty the breasts after the nursing session is over makes no sense, because breasts produce milk continuously.
- To check if there is milk proper expressing is needed. Expressing milk is an art to be learnt and the first times you might be able to extract only few drops. This does not mean that you have no milk. You are simply not being able to express it. You will know if you have milk if your baby swallows while nursing, if he wets enough nappies and he grows in weight.
- We often check if milk is still good by careful examination.

Whatever is the look of mother milk, it is always adequate for that particular baby.

_{(Source: *L'arte dell'allattamento materno*, La Leche League Publications, 2003, pp. 359-363).}

Manual expression

Manual expression can be done everywhere at no cost. It is always available and it ensures maximum level of sterility. It is especially useful in case of occasional need or to relief the tension of a full breast. Remember to wash your hands carefully before starting and collect the milk in a clean container.

Avoid squeezing your breast. Place your thumb on one side of the areola and the rest of the fingers on the opposite side. Fingers should be placed between 2.5 and 4 cm from the nipple, according to the dimension of the areola. After pushing the whole breast towards your chest, gently press your fingers up and down to express the milk. Keep rotating the position of your fingers around the areola, in order to empty all the ducts. To facilitate the flow, shift breast approximately every five minutes.

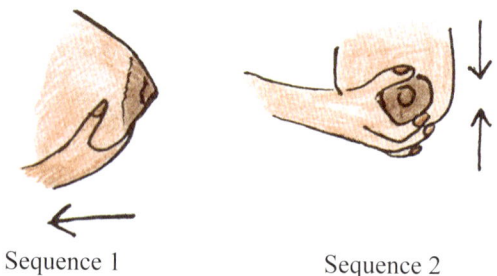

Sequence 1   Sequence 2

Pumps

There are different kinds of breast pumps. These are useful in case you need to express bigger quantities of milk or if you do not feel at ease with manual expression.

Manual pumps are good for sporadic usage. Avoid syringe-like pumps because they can damage the nipple.

Electric pumps are useful in case you need to express your milk more frequently. They come in different dimensions and there are different models available on the market. The bigger models (they can express milk even from both breasts simultaneously) are useful in case you need to express your milk very frequently (for *example,* premature babies, temporary interruption of breastfeeding).

Tips to facilitate milk expression

Be in a quiet, private space, relax, take your time. Look at your baby or at your baby's picture. Smell him or a blanket or cloth with his odor. Touch your baby, if he is there.

Massage your breast gently, bend your chest forward and gently shake your breasts with your hands. You may take a hot bath or warm water applications before expressing.

How to preserve and use expressed milk

At room temperature (up to 24 °C) you can preserve the milk for ten hours.

In the fridge you can preserve it for three days provided that there are no excessive blackouts and voltage variations.

Again, the milk can be preserved in a freezer up to three months with temperature between -5 and -15 °C (again no blackouts, etc.). Take care of placing the milk far from the door. It can be preserved for 6 months in a freezer with temperature -19 °C.

Always defreeze the milk gradually, by leaving it at room temperature or putting the container in warm water. Never microwave it as this could kill important substances contained in it. Do not heat the milk excessively. Babies are used to drink it at our body temperature. Throw the defrozen milk after 24 hours.

(Source: Tiziana Catanzani, Paola Negri, Allattare un gesto d'amore, Bonomi, 2005, pp.143-144).

Special Circumstances

Twins

Having twins requires particular life-organization arrangements as everything is *double*. It is important to be prepared since pregnancy and to put particular care in organizing our network of helpers, so that we can get the maximum time with our babies to learn breastfeeding.

Leave house-hold chores aside for a while and take your time. Try to rest as much as you can when your babies rest.

Breastfeeding twins might be tiring and sometimes difficult at the beginning but it is possible and it can be source of immense satisfaction. If you are worried whether you will be able to produce enough milk, always keep in mind that breastfeeding is ruled by the law of demand and supply. If you nurse your babies whenever they ask for it, your milk supply will be perfectly adequate. Women have been successfully breastfeeding twins, triplets, and more!

You may decide to nurse your babies one at a time or together at the same time. In any case, there will be circumstances in which your babies will need to nurse at the same time.

Here are two examples of tandem

From BPNI's Training Material "Infant and Young Child Feeding Counseling: A Training Course - The 3 in 1 course"

Special Circumstances

nursing positions where both babies are held in a 'rugby hold' and both babies held in a 'cradle hold' (crossing each other).

These are not the only two possibilities. You can mix the two positions, having one baby in a cradle hold and the other in a rugby hold. Or you can lie down supine with one baby per side, both supported by pillows.

Be creative, find what works best for you, having care to make your children nurse from both sides. Make yourself comfortable by using as many pillows and supports you need. You may find the use of a nursing pillow very helpful. You can easily make it by yourself or with the help of a tailor, if you do not want to buy it ready made.

Nursing pillow

Pregnancy and tandem nursing

Breastfeeding during pregnancy has no risks unless abort menaces have happened or there are signs of possible premature delivery. Many

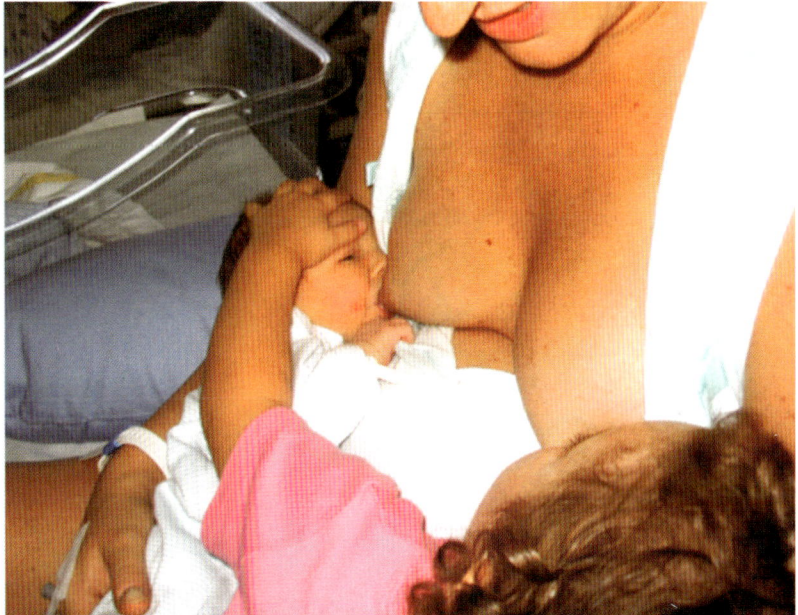

Manuela with Irene and Carolina.

mothers all over the world breastfeed during pregnancy. They simply find it natural. There is nothing wrong with that. Some children will wean spontaneously, if they are ready during the last trimester when milk becomes colostrum and changes its taste. Some others will go on nursing and they will keep nursing with their new siblings. This makes their bond very strong and reduces jealousy. Imagine, it might so happen that the elder child will most probably conserve the memory of this tandem nursing during adulthood! Some mothers will be okay with nursing during pregnancy and tandem nursing as well. Some others might not like it. They might find this double suction unpleasant and opt for nursing one child at a time or they might feel the need to wean the elder. It is fine. It has to be an individual choice. We suggest that weaning should happen gradually and with all the love and care of the mother (see: *Weaning*).

Tandem nursing arrangements for children of different ages will be similar to twins tandem nursing positions.

Caesarian and operative deliveries

Babies might be sleepy during the first hours or days of life as an effect of anesthetics. This might make their suction weak and not well coordinated for sometime. Learning breastfeeding might require patience. Nevertheless it does not mean that you will not be able to breastfeed successfully.

Try to breastfeed immediately after birth, as if you had a natural delivery. This means that, when possible, you should prefer local anesthesia to a general one. It will also give you the opportunity to *live* through the birth procedure consciously. In case this is not possible, ask to breastfeed your baby as you wake up.

During the first days you might be more comfortable breastfeeding your baby from a lying down position. Until your cut heals a bit you might need some help to place your baby and move him from one side to the other. Note that it is important that you feed the baby from both the breasts, in order to avoid engorgements and ensure adequate milk supply.

If you feed your baby while sitting, support him/her with a pillow and make sure to keep him/her at your breast level. This will help you avoid excessive efforts and it will protect your abdomen.

Premature babies

Premature babies are all different from one another. They come in different weights and according to this they might or might not be able to suck from the breast at birth. Some of them are particularly weak and might be hospitalized for a month or more. They might need to be fed with a special device which is inserted in their mouth and reaches their stomach directly. Whatever is the circumstance, even babies who cannot suck from the breast can be fed your expressed milk and colostrum. This is very important because it gives the mother a sense of purpose and fills the gap created by the forced separation. But even more important it is because of the nutritional value of the mother's milk. If this is the perfect food for any newborn, even more so it is for the premature babies. They are in extreme need of the immunity protection that comes with breastfeeding. Furthermore, it has been scientifically proven that the milk and colostrum produced by mothers of premature babies is different in its composition from that of other mothers. It contains *exactly* the kind of nutrients that premature babies especially need to survive and grow!

Kangaroo care

Premature babies and their mothers gain a lot of benefit by spending time skin to skin just like marsupials! Mother and baby can be both wrapped in a sweater or a shirt. It has been seen that premature babies who are kept skin to skin with their mothers spend more time in a state of calm alertness and thrive better than those left in the incubator. This frequent touch with her baby might also ease for the mother the task of expressing milk. Ask the hospital personnel to try this practice, as soon as your baby is considered ready for it.

Newborn jaundice

Newborn jaundice indicates an increase of bilirubin, which can be stored in babies tissues instead of being eliminated. This gives the characteristic yellow-golden color to the skin and eyes. We can distinguish three kinds of jaundice:

Physiologic jaundice

It is a very common phenomenon. Newborn babies have higher levels of red globules in their blood because of the limited presence of oxygen inside the uterus. After birth they are no more necessary in such big quantity and they need to be eliminated. Bilirubin is a residual of their elimination process. When bilirubin is not totally expelled though feces, it is stored in babies' tissues.

This condition is normal and innocuous and there is no reason to worry in case of a healthy newborn. It normally appears between the second and the fourth day after birth and disappears within one to three weeks. Breastfeeding frequently and immediately after birth helps eliminating bilirubin, so it prevents and cures jaundice as mother milk and especially colostrum have a laxative effect. Remember that bilirubin is eliminated through feces, not through urine! Giving the baby water in order to 'wash' the jaundice away has no use and it is a wrong practice because it interferes with the frequency of breastfeeding.

'Mother milk' jaundice or late jaundice

It appears only five-seven days after birth and can last up to ten weeks. It is again an innocuous phenomenon. Breastfeeding should not be interrupted, not even temporarily, in order to distinguish such kind of jaundice from the pathologic one. There are other ways to diagnose pathologic jaundice. Interrupting breastfeeding (even for one day) during the first crucial days can compromise the success of breastfeeding. Furthermore, breastfeeding is the best way to eliminate bilirubin and the best cure for newborn jaundice.

Pathologic jaundice

It can be due to abnormal destruction of red globules, poor liver functioning or any other cause of increased bilirubin levels, like infections, metabolic problems, gastro intestinal occlusions. In this case bilirubin levels become very high and very rapidly. This could create cerebral damages, although they do not occur that frequently. The baby might need to be cured normally with phototherapy. Even in this case breastfeeding should continue and in fact, it helps to solve the problem to a great extent. The mother must not be separated from her baby and she must be given the right to breastfeed him at least every two hours (ten to twelve times within 24 hours).

The success of phototherapy is not undermined by these frequent interruptions. In some cases phototherapy can be done at home. There are lamps that can be installed at home and nowadays even special optic fiber blankets in which to wrap the baby have been invented. If you decide to treat your baby at home, you will just have to keep taking him to the hospital for regular blood testing and check-ups.

Newborn hypoglycemia

The best prevention and treatment to bring newborn's sugar levels to normality is breastfeeding them frequently, immediately after birth. Breastfeeding means frequent small meals rich in proteins to be given to the patient which is exactly the same therapy recommended to adults who suffer from similar problems. Glucose solutions are often counterproductive because they create a sudden raise in blood sugars, followed by drastic drops. The practice of giving glucose water to any newborn below a certain weight is wrong. You should discuss this issue with hospital personnel before delivering. Some babies who are overweight at birth might be prone to it. If a real emergency arises and there is a real necessity to give the baby glucose water, artificial nipples should not be used. Good alternatives are spoons, small cups, syringes, droppers.

Hypoglycemia, if it happens, should be managed under specialist care.

Genetic and metabolic problems

Babies with genetic and metabolic problems (or any other kind of health problems) need breastfeeding and mother's touch even more than others. They derive a lot of benefit from breastfeeding. There is no need to avoid it. Even in case the baby has to be hospitalized or undergo surgical operations, mothers and babies have the right not be separated and to carry on the breastfeeding. In case of surgery, you will probably have to find out how much time the baby should fast before the operation.

With a bit of patience and help (initially you may need the support of a lactation consultant) you can breastfeed successfully even babies with specific problems related to their mouth and tongue like babies with tight frenulum and babies with labioschisis and palatoschisis. Such conditions might require surgical intervention too.

When the Mother has Medical Problems

Most mothers' medical problems are compatible with breastfeeding and in fact breastfeeding brings benefits to both mother and baby. Exclusive breastfeeding for the first six months is now even advised in case of HIV, as it is protective against the transmission of the virus. It does carry a minimal risk of transmission from the mother to the baby but it has been seen that mixed feeding is much more risky. In case of HIV, rather than mixed feeding, it is better to go exclusively for artificial feeding. Breastfeeding is not advised in case of drugs and substance abuse or absolute necessity of medication which are not compatible with breastfeeding. Remember, though in case of common diseases nowadays it is almost always possible to find alternative medications which are suitable for breastfeeding mother. Discuss this with your doctor and if needed, search for different opinions. A lactation consultant will be able to guide you regarding this matter.

CHART 9
MEDICATIONS WHICH SHOULD BE AVOIDED DURING BREASTFEEDING:

Ergotamine (anti-migraine), cyclosporine, methotrexate, doxorubicin, cyclophosphamide (cytotoxic and antitumor drugs), heroine, morphine, cocaine, amphetamines, sulphamides, tetracycline antibiotics (if used for longer than three weeks), cloramphenicol (antibiotics), bromocriptine (cure of galactorrhea and prolactinoma), radioactive contrast methods (in this case the mother should temporary interrupt breastfeeding–milk can be expressed and thrown to prevent engorgement and maintain the production), amiodarone (heart problems).

(Source: Tiziana Catanzani, Paola Negri, *Allattare un gesto d'amore*, Bonomi, 2005, pp. 247-248)

Ready for the First Complementary Foods

When is the right time?
The World Health Organization recommends exclusive breastfeeding for at least six months when not even water or herbal teas are to be given to the child. NOTHING else other than mother's milk should be given!

Signs to watch out for
There are a few signs which will tell you that your baby is ready for the first complementary foods when

- The baby can sit without support
- The baby can actively use his hands to bring food to his mouth
- The baby has the capacity to refuse food if he does not want it
- When you place some food on the edge of the baby's tongue, he pulls his tongue backwards in his mouth. This is a spontaneous reflex which indicates that the baby is ready for solids. Sucking requires in fact the opposite tongue movement. If a baby is not ready for solids, whatever you place on his tongue will be thrown out. In this case there is no point insisting. It is better to wait sometimes till your baby is ready.
- The baby makes chewing-like movement with his jaws when he has food in his mouth and his gums are hard enough to chew. Ideally, he should also have some teeth. All mammals start eating other foods other than mother's milk after the first teeth appear (this indicate a certain maturity of the digestive system also).
- The baby shows active interest and curiosity about trying adults' food

Complementing, not substituting!

Breastfeeding is not simply providing nutrition, it is love and comfort. Breastfed babies do not have tight schedule for nursing and in fact they do not 'eat meals' but 'they nurse'. It makes no sense trying to substitute nursing with solids. The baby will not be more eager to eat solid foods because he is hungry. Indeed, it is the opposite. Nobody is in the mood to explore when they are starving. Furthermore, hunger is a bad counselor. The baby might accept things that he would otherwise refuse. This should not happen. Babies have an extremely good capacity to self regulate. They refuse what is bad for them at that particular moment. It is a powerful protection mechanism against alimentary allergies and intolerances and there should not be interferences with it. New foods should always be presented after nursing, not before and absolutely not *instead* of nursing. This way to go about it is also a warranty that your child is getting enough nutrition from breastfeeding and will keep your milk supply high. If you are so worried about times and schedules, you can keep breastfeeding your baby on demand and let him try solids when the rest of the family is eating.

What are the right foods?

Every culture has its own ways of initiating a child into eating solid food. Children grow well all over the world, may they be given vegetables, fruits, lentils or chicken soup as their first food.

If you avoid industrial foods, sweets and junks and follow the very old tradition of your geographic area, it will be better for your child. Choose fresh, nutritious vegetables, cereals, fruits. Go for natural and organic fruits and vegetables, if they are available.

If you wait for the child to be ready for solids, there is no need for baby foods and homogenized products. These were initially meant for sick and elderly people. During the boom of industrialization they have been turned into baby foods, in order to feed babies with solids more and more precociously. Baby foods are expensive and they not needed in case of healthy babies who are ready for solids.

When the child eats solids, he will also need water. You do not need bottles for this purpose. A seeping cup or a small glass will serve the purpose quite nicely.

Let your little explorer explore by himself, if he wants. There is nothing wrong if he touches the food with his hands. Let him get dirty, let him mess up. All these are important for his growth.

Avoid starting with potentially allergenic foods (see: *Mother's nutrition*). Always give the baby small amounts of a new food and wait one week before introducing another one. If you do not observe any reaction, go ahead.

And remember: there is no need to rush – not even if the neighbors' baby eats more or looks bigger! Not even if our gossiping friends tell us that our baby looks weak. Learn to trust your child and your instincts!

A note about allergies and intolerances

Children who are prone to have alimentary allergies and intolerances tend to refuse solids for longer time. Let them breastfeed for long. It is the best protection that you can give them. You are not in a hurry.

The later you introduce allergenic foods, the less likely allergies will appear. You should keep this in mind especially if you or any other family member is suffering from allergies or if your baby has shown signs of allergy or intolerance to foods that were present in your diet (see: *Mother's nutrition*).

Breastfeeding Older Children

Although it is no more so in today's industrialized societies, breastfeeding toddlers (and even older children) has been the norm for centuries and in many traditional societies it is still so.

There is nothing wrong with this practice, as long as the mother and the baby enjoy it. Prolonged breastfeeding increases health benefits for both mother and her child. The first is more protected from diseases like cancer and osteoporosis, the second keeps receiving immunity protection and good nutrients. It is not true that milk looses its nutritional value (we are often told that 'it becomes like water') after some time. Indeed, it adapts its composition to the actual needs of the baby, according to his growth stage. Breastfeeding older children has other several emotional and health benefits. It is a powerful mean to reassure a scared or hurt child, to console him or to calm his tantrums. When the baby is sick and refuses all food and drink, he will rarely refuse breast. Breastfeeding a sick child can sometimes prove to be a real blessing! It will ensure that his nutritional needs are satisfied.

Elena with Caterina

Weaning

Weaning is a slow process and it happens sooner or later. Children wean gradually and spontaneously. There is no need to put limitations or to fix schedules. Natural weaning is the best way to go about it. Children's need to nurse reduces while other life experiences become more important for them.

Nevertheless, in case the mother feels the need to speed up the process, we suggest to avoid going about it abruptly, with questionable methods like leaving the child alone for one or more nights or covering the nipple with spices or dark colors. This will make him feel abandoned. This is a critical moment for him, and he needs your comfort. He needs to know that you are still there for him!

Instead of trying the above methods, try to distract the child. Do

not let him get bored; offer him healthy snacks and drinks to prevent his hunger and thirst and avoid showing him your breasts. This will help you to increase the distance between one nursing and the next. You can also reduce their duration by telling your child that you will nurse only the time needed to count till ten or to sing a song or read a story. Generally children accept this and it works. You can also tell your child that you will nurse only during particular moments (for example, before sleeping or when he wakes up perhaps). During the night you can tell him that you will nurse when the sun will rise.

Breastfeeding is ultimately love and with love it should end… Like it started. Do not be in a hurry: you will never get those days back.

Bibliography

Carlos Gonzales, *Il mio bambino non mi mangia. Consigli per prevenire e risolvere il problema*, Bonomi, 2003.

Jack Newman, Teresa Pitman, *The Ultimate Breastfeeding Book of Answers. The most comprehensive problem-solution guide to Breastfeeding from the foremost expert in North America*, Prima, 2000.

Janet Balaskas, Yehudi Gordon, *Avremo un bambino*, Red, 1989.

La Leche League International, *L'arte dell'allattamento materno*, LLLI, 2005.

La Leche League International, *The Womanly Art of Breastfeeding*, LLLI, 1958.

La Leche League International, *Allattamento al seno. Il libro delle risposte*, vol. 1-2, LLI, 1991.

La Leche League International, *Svezzamento, passo dopo passo*, LLLI, 2008.

Lino Del Pup, *Alimentazione in gravidanza e allattamento. Consigli pratici per la salute e il benessere della madre e del bambino*, Editeam, 2006.

Norma Jane Bumgarner, *Mothering Your Nursing Toddler*, LLLI, 2000.

Tiziana Catanzani, Paola Negri, *Allattare un gesto d'amore. Come vivere con serenità l'esperienza dell'allattamento*, Bonomi, 2005.

Tiziana Valpiana, *L'alimentazione naturale del bambino. Allattamento, svezzamento, ricette salutari fino ai sei anni*, Red, 1988.

William Sears, *Night time parenting. How to get your baby and child to sleep*, LLLI, 1999.

William and Martha Sears, *The Baby Book. Everything you need to know about your baby from birth to age two*, Thorsons, 2005.

William and Martha Sears, *Allattamento e svezzamento*, Red, 2003.